FL✦RENCE
A TRAVELER'S GUIDE to its
GEMS & GIANTS

PATTY CIVALLERI

1-TAKE MultiMedia
6216 Pacific Coast Hwy, #321
Long Beach, Ca 90803
Email: Pubs@1Take.com
FlorenceTravelBook.com

ISBN: 978-0-9981926-0-4

Modern and outdoor photography by Patty Civalleri.
All other photos are courtesy of Open Source, Creative Commons and Adobe Stock.
Cover design and layout by Patty Civalleri.

To Captain Roger, the best friend I have ever had, and will ever have. Your indefatigable support of my incessant array of projects has more meaning to me than you will ever know.

"Stendhalismo"
("Stendhal Syndrome")

UrbanDictonary.com defines this condition as follows:
"When someone is so impressed and in awe of something of artistic value that they start to show maniacal symptoms. Patients sometimes even become aggressive."

WordSpy.com defines this condition as
"n. Dizziness, panic, paranoia, or madness caused by viewing certain artistic or historical artifacts or by trying to see too many such artifacts in too short a time."

Warning:
Florence, Italy is known to be the hot-bed of
the Stendhal Syndrome.

Cure: The only known way to cure this hideous disease is to read this book. It will demystify the complexity of Florence, the most artistic city in the world, so that you will return home with 'calm eyes' and a higher I.Q.

Humanism

as defined by Dictionary.com

hu·man·ism
(H)YOO-meh-niz-em

Noun: an outlook or system of thought attaching prime importance to human rather than divine or supernatural matters. Humanist beliefs stress the potential value and goodness of human beings, emphasize common human needs, and seek solely rational ways of solving human problems.

The Rediscovery of the Human Spirit.

DECIDE FOR YOURSELF

Do you know what you want to do & see in Florence?
Here are some clues to point you in a direction that will help you to see more of what's fun for you - without wasting your short time on the fluff that everyone thinks you SHOULD see.

_____ Who punched Michelangelo in the nose? *p119*

_____ Who ignited the original Bonfire of the Vanities? *p112*

_____ Who was the Pirate pope? *p34*

_____ What famous artist was kidnapped and sold into slavery? *p92*

_____ Was Michelangelo's "Sleeping Cupid" a fake? *p121*

_____ Were the Medici the first Mafia Family? *p48*

_____ Who used a Plague Mask? Why? *p18*

_____ How to make a bronze sculpture in 7 easy steps *p97*

_____ Why was Lorenzo so Magnificent? *p40*

_____ Where was the first martyr, San Miniato, beheaded? *p227*

_____ Who could be considered to be the "Entrepreneur" of the Renaissance? *p116*

_____ Who is considered to be the Father of the Italian language? *p54*

_____ Where should you go to take the BEST PHOTOS of the whole city? *p234*

_____ Who created the "Gates to Paradise?" Who gave them that nickname? *p166*

_____ Where did Botticelli get this nickname? *p98*

_____ What is hidden on the back of Cellini's statue of "Perseus"? *p139*

_____ Who executed the Mad Monk? *p114*

_____ What secrets are hidden in Medici's bedroom closet in the Palazzo Vecchio? *p174*

_____ Why was the mysterious Vasari Corridor (tunnel) built ABOVE the ground? *p200*

_____ Who is considered to be the "Bad Boy" of the Renaissance? *p138*

_____ How many 'David' statues were famous in Florence BEFORE Michelangelo created his own famous David? Who created them? Where are they now? *p128*

_____ Who is buried in Basilica di Santa Croce? *p204*

_____ What famous astronomer 'performed tricks' in the Medici court? *p148*

_____ Why was the church of Santa Maria del Fiore an embarrassment to the city? *p69, p158*

_____ Who was the 'womanizer' of the Renaissance? *p132*

⚜

_____ What secret signs are hidden in plain sight on the streets of Florence? *p246*

_____ What little boy found David's broken arm and kept it hidden until adulthood? *p145*

_____ Who broke Dante's heart? *p57*

_____ From Cartoon to Fresco in 4 simple steps *p110*

_____ Why is Machiavelli so misunderstood? *p117*

_____ What Maestro swore he would never paint again after seeing a young student paint for the first time? Who was that student? *p97*

_____ What 2 enemies were imprisoned in the same Palazzo Vecchio cell ~ 50 years apart? *p178*

_____ What scientist was imprisoned, tortured and exiled during the Roman Inquisition? *p150*

_____ Where can you buy the potions and elixirs mixed for nearly 1000 yrs for the wealthy? *p220*

_____ Who caused Royal Embarrassment by giving Queen Victoria a gift? *p217*

_____ What church has an astronomical measuring device (quadrant) in its exterior wall? *p219*

_____ What was the oval-shaped track outside of Santa Maria Novella used for? *p218*

_____ Who was the 'Bird Man' of the Renaissance? *p86*

_____ What is an "illuminator?" *p82*

_____ Who hid people's hands in his paintings because he couldn't make them look real? *p93*

_____ Who made it fashionable for little girls to wear garlands of flowers in their hair? *p102*

_____ Where can you go to find the best street art in the world? *p244*

_____ Where will you find ancient Etruscan and Roman archaeological ruins? *p249*

_____ What is a great path for runners to follow around the city? *p226*

_____ Why was a fig leaf used to cover the genitals on sculptures and in paintings?

_____ Whose family assembled his machines and created a museum about him? *p208*

Bragging Rights...

Did you find more fun stories and mysteries that were left behind by these fantastic Renaissance Giants? We want to know what/where they are.

Visit our Website http://FlorenceTravelBook.com, and in an email, tell us all about the mysteries that you found. If you give us permission, we will happily give you credit for that clue if we use it in the next edition of this book - and you'll have bragging rights!

TABLE OF CONTENTS

TABLE OF CONTENTS

The People

(in the order of their birth.)

VISUAL TABLE OF CONTENTS

 The 5 "Giants" who demonstrated that change was surely afoot were Brunelleschi, Donatello, Ghiberti, Uccello, and Masaccio.

Member of the House of Medici - the wealthy family behind it all.

The Places
they left behind

il Duomo   *p158*

Santa Maria del Fiore *p162*

Baptistery *p164*

Gates to Paradise *p166*

Giotto's Bell Tower (Campanile) *p168*

Uffizi Gallery *p170*

Accademia *p172*

Palazzo Vecchio   *p174*

Ponte Vecchio *p180*

Palazzo Pitti (Pitti Palace) *p184*

Boboli Gardens *p186*

Grotto di Buontalenti *p188*

Wandering
Around Today

Walls & Doors (with map) *p226*

What's a Piazza? *p228*

Camera buffs, THIS is for YOU!

Getting High in Florence *p234*

The Arno River *p240*

How could the Renaissance have occurred first in Florence? Why didn't it start elsewhere?

A variety of circumstances had to be in play simultaneously, each adding its own timber to a growing flame which ultimately became The Renaissance.

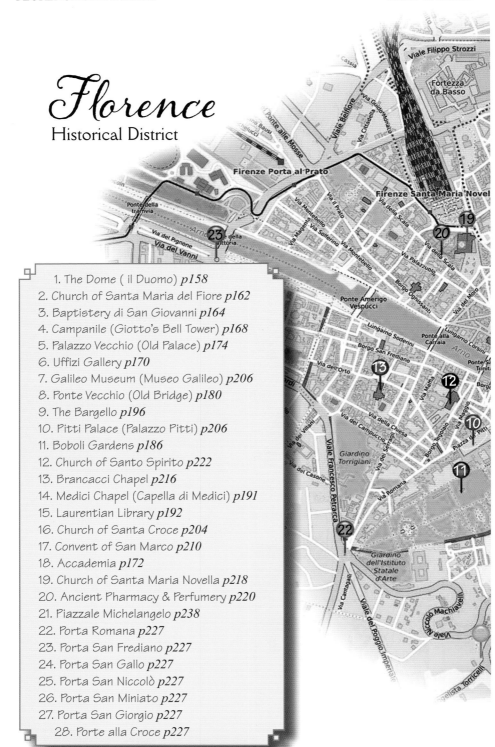

Florence
Historical District

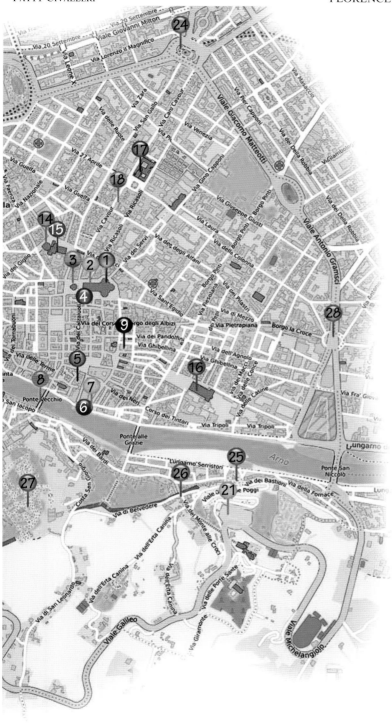

The Plague Doctor

During the time of the Black Plague, it was thought that the foul odors that emanated from a patient or the foul air pollution caused by the internal rotting of a diseased person, were the causes of the disease. This was known as the Miasma Theory. This thinking however, was ultimately displaced by Germ Theory.

The plague doctor costume was a common sight during the 14th century. The wide-brimmed hat identified its wearer as a doctor ~ similar to the white coat worn by medical professionals today. The long bulky coat was worn as a layer of protection over their regular clothes. The lengthy beak of the glass-eyed mask was filled with herbs and dried flowers to combat the offensive odors, all-the-while serving to keep the doctor at a safe distance from the patient. The beak may have been filled with any combination of rose petals, camphor, mint, carnations and lavender to both ward off the bad air and to provide pleasing and hopefully preventative aromas. The stick was a pointing devise that the doctor used to point to different parts of the patient's body without having to get too close.

The appearance of a plague doctor in your town would invoke the fear of doom in even the most stalwart of heart and health.

Today, visitors to Florence enjoy a varied assortment of mask shops. Among the fun 'Carnivale' masks, these frightening plague masks can be found as well.

BACKGROUND

INTRODUCTION

How did Florence, with her tiny college-sized population of 35,000 produce a never-before-seen number of actual geniuses? Take a look through this vastly incomplete list of names. You may not know more than a smidgen about any of them, but their legends have been echoed in the winds of history for 600 years.

By themselves, only a couple of these folks made a significant dent, mostly in the finite world of art. But combined? They were **the thundering voice that changed all of Western history.**

Michelangelo * Dante * Brunelleschi * da Vinci * Donatello * Galileo
Botticelli * Machiavelli * Cellini * Raphael * Verrocchio
Ghiberti * Giotto * Della Robbia * Masaccio * Michelozzo
Lippi * Vasari * Uccello * Petrarch * Angelico
...and behind them all loomed the House of Medici.

The Renaissance sprang from the sickening stench that was the Bubonic Plague, aka the Black Death, and the Black Plague. The plague swept through with a raging anger from the east in the mid-1300's, and after three years, over 60% of the population of Europe, North Africa and the Middle East had been eliminated.

Springing from the mire of the plague is one thing. But how could this tiny walled-in town of Florence yield this many giants - virtually all at once? After all, the plague devastated vast amounts of people throughout Europe, North Africa and the Middle East. But afterwards, none of the other cities in those places magically produced a group of men who, with no prior intention to do so, changed nearly everything in the Western World. Not even Rome, with her much larger and more varied population, produced this cast of Giants.

So again: Why Florence? Why all at once?

Giorgio Vasari, an insightful 16th century Florentine writer, coined the term "Renaissance" to describe this quirk of history. "Renaissance" is a French word meaning "rebirth."

With the picture in your mind of the mass devastation caused by the bubonic plague, combined with the walled-in, mind-numbing, God-fearing lifestyle that was the Dark Ages, I would like to introduce you to this sudden blooming of godlike geniuses who sprang from this little town of Florence in an uproarious awakening called The Renaissance.

This book will tell the tales of those impassioned men that through their own substantive genius, coupled with a healthy amount of creativity, and doused with plenty of long-suppressed curiosity, they managed to yank the entire world into what has become known as as the Renaissance period.

BACKGROUND

ARTISTS

Michelangelo
Da Vinci   Botticelli   Donatello
Lippi   Brunelleschi   Cellini   Vasari
Ghiberti   Michelozzo   Masaccio
Galileo   Raphael   Verocchio
Uccello   Giotto   Della Robbia
Petrarch   Ghirlandaio   Fra Angelico

ARCHITECTS

Michelangelo
Vasari   Da Vinci   Raphael
Brunelleschi   Giotto
Michelozzo   Ghiberti

SCIENTISTS

Da Vinci   Galileo
Brunelleschi

THINKERS

Galileo   Dante
Vasari   Macchiavelli
Petrarch   Da Vinci
Poggio

**Renaissance Era
1400 - 1600
Florence**

The Medici Bank was started by Giovanni de'Medici and eventually became the biggest bank in all of Europe. The Medici money, their Vatican connections and their personal love for the arts and literature came together to create this explosion of free-thinking that was expressed through art, architecture, science literature and philosophy.

These were merely a few of the 'Giants' whose lives were touched by the Medici in one way or another, and who made the biggest contributions to the Renaissance. But there were hundreds more incredible people that helped to shape this explosive transition from the Middle Ages into the enlightened Renaissance Era.

GANGSTERS · TYRANTS · ART · THIEVES · POLITICS · GREED · ARCHIT... · MAGNIFIC... · SCIENCE · MURDER

House of Medici

Giovanni
di Bicci de' Medici
Created the Bank

Cosimo
"the Elder"
Ruled: early 1400's

Lorenzo
"the Magnificent"
Ruled: late 1400's

Cosimo I
Grand Duke of Tuscany
Ruled: mid 1500's

These Medici were the most influential during the Renaissance period. Other Medici descendants ruled off-and-on until 1735 when the House of Medici was considered to have ended.

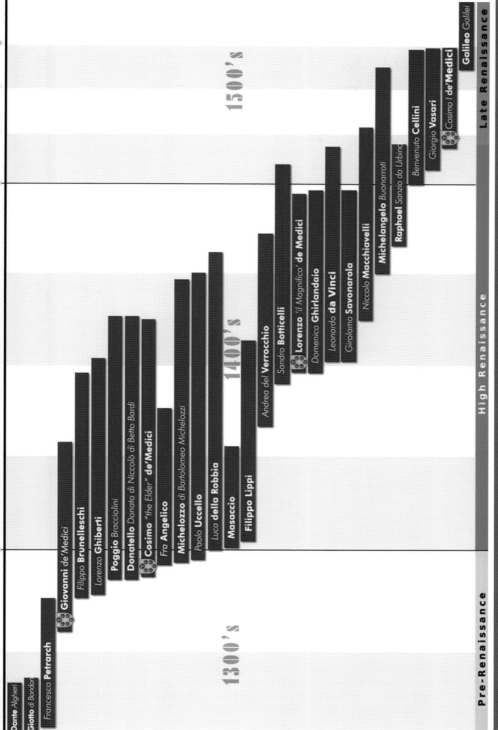

BACKGROUND

Late Renaissance · High Renaissance · Pre-Renaissance

Galileo Galilei
Cosimo I de'Medici
Giorgio Vasari
Benvenuto Cellini
Raphael Sanzio da Urbino
Michelangelo Buonarroti
Niccolò Macchiavelli
Girolamo Savonarola
Leonardo da Vinci
Domenico Ghirlandaio
Lorenzo 'il Magnifico' de Medici
Sandro Botticelli
Andrea del Verrocchio
Filippo Lippi
Masaccio
Luca della Robbia
Paolo Uccello
Michelozzo di Bartolomeo Michelozzi
Fra Angelico
Cosimo "the Elder" de'Medici
Donatello Donato di Niccolò di Betto Bardi
Poggio Bracciolini
Lorenzo Ghiberti
Filippo Brunelleschi
Giovanni de'Medici
Francesco Petrarch
Giotto di Bondone
Dante Alighieri

1500's · 1400's · 1300's

BACKGROUND

WHAT'S A RENAISSANCE?
FROM DARKNESS INTO THE LIGHT

Life before the renaissance: the dark ages

After the Black Plague (mid-1300's; *pg"The Plague Doctor" on page 18*) exterminated nearly 60% of the people in Europe, North Africa and the Middle East, hundreds of disparate towns and cities spent decades mourning their massive losses. Eventually, the process of mourning gave way to the 'rebooting' of life. At this point, several events merged simultaneously to create an epic avalanche of change. It was powerful enough to transform Western Europe from the primordial ooze that was the murky servitude of the Middle Ages into the enlightened 'rebirth' we have come to know as the Renaissance.

Life in the Florentine Middle Ages (before)

During the Middle Ages, there was no 'Italy' as we know it today. Instead, spread all around 'the boot' were a collection of City-States that were each self-governing. Florence was one of these City-States ruled by a combination of moneyed families, the Church, and thugs.

Life in Florence during the Middle Ages was, by modern standards, extremely limited in scope. Citizens lived within high walls for their protection. There were no books, pamphlets or reading materials of any kind. Therefore, there wasn't very much - if any - exposure to new thoughts or ideas from the outside world, let alone from ancient history. From birth, citizens knew only what they were told by either the Church or by whichever 'bully' was in power at any given moment - or by both. This complete filtering of information gave the leaders total control over the population. For example, it was not uncommon that folks were told that every single waking moment was to be dedicated to the church, God or to the civic benefit. There was no 'I' ~ merely a collective consciousness.

Superstition was a useful governing tool. For example, leaving the city walls was frowned upon and thereby controlled with the help of stories and legends of the monsters and ogres that waited in the forests for people to leave the city, and that would eat them if they did. (The fact that 'Ogres especially loved children' ingrained these dangers at an early age.) Keeping a population inside of the walls and controlling all information was a great way to run things in your favor - if indeed you happened to be a civic ruler or a high member of the church. But still, there were leaks.

Being a Republic, citizens of Florence could actually elect their own leaders. To be considered a 'citizen' you had to formally belong to a 'guild'. Each guild specialized in a particular type of business. For example, there was a Wool Guild, a Sheepherders Guild, a Silk Guild, a Goldsmiths Guild, etc. These guilds offered a system of apprenticeship and training to the local youth in order to maintain a continuous flow of goods and services. The guilds also controlled the manufacture and distribution of these goods and services, as well as the taxation of any income produced by the distribution of these goods and services.

The arts were encouraged provided that the artists produced items that were for the benefit of the Church or for creatively emphasizing the stories of the Bible. Paintings had to all maintain a theme from the Bible; music and poetry were limited to songs of everyday life and to stories of the Bible. The strumming of a lute or a poetic biblical recitation could often be heard as you walked down the dirt and stone alleyways of old Florence. And yet, some were quietly rebellious in nature.

BACKGROUND

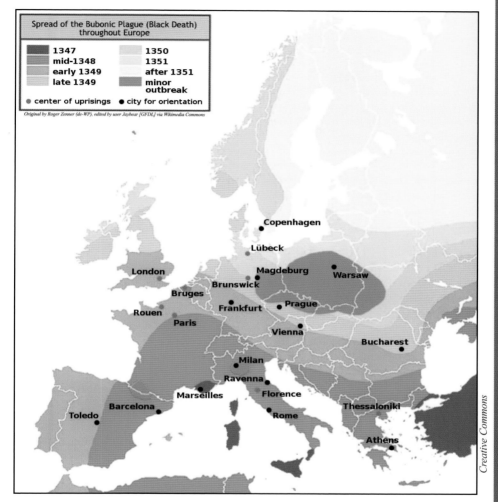

Spread of the Bubonic Plague (Black Death) throughout Europe

- 1347
- mid-1348
- early 1349
- late 1349
- 1350
- 1351
- after 1351
- minor outbreak
- center of uprisings ● city for orientation

Original by Roger Zenner (de-WP), edited by user Jaybear [GFDL] via Wikimedia Commons

Creative Commons

People had no deep knowledge of history, other than what they were told. They did not know that over 1,000 years before them, there existed rich cultures with complex political systems, mathematics, art, science, fantastic architecture, thought-provoking literature and influences from around the world. We know these cultures as the Greeks and the Roman (and even the Egyptian) Empires. But most of Western Europe during the Middle Ages had no awareness of those ancient cultures. They simply knew that life had always been the same for all time before. But still, there were leaks.

So how did all of this change? Here comes the Renaissance!

Mid-1300's

Let's begin with the "The Plague Doctor" p18 in Florence as our starting point. During the plague, people did many things to escape this black disease. They fled into the forest with the hopes of avoiding the plague that was exploding inside of the walls. Once in the forest, they began to meet people from other areas, some of whom had travelled to faraway places such as Rome, or to the strange lands of France or Spain or Germany. These newly-encountered people carried with them incredible tales and an unheard-of spirit of adventure. Locals were encouraged to think about the bigger world and to question the knowledge of the only world they knew. A Florentine curiosity was born.

A small but growing group of elite and schooled Florentines discovered a few ancient writings that were over 1,000 years old. The documents they found were written by unfamiliar names like Socrates, Plato, Lucretius and Cicero. Our little group of Florentines were catapulted into whole new ways of thinking. And they hungered for more. A few of them, such as Petrarch and Poggio Bracciolini, boarded their donkeys and rode hundreds of miles into the hills and mountains of Germany and France in search of the quiet monasteries that hid libraries within their walls. This is where so many of these ancient writings had been concealed from literate eyes for over a millennium. These writings spewed forth such odd concepts such as free-thinking, creativity, questioning and the importance of human individualism. A fellow named Petrarch coined the term 'Humanism' to describe this collection of concepts. And we all know that once you give name to a concept, it becomes easier to sell.

Late 1300's ~ The Leaks

There was a fellow named Giovanni de' Medici who started a little lending business in the back room of his family's wool shop. This Medici fellow did something that was unheard-of in the existing elite financial circles: he lent money to the lower classes, enabling them to begin to stand on their own. There was another fellow who was known to roam the streets of Florence spouting such things as "think for yourself" and "question everything" to anyone that would listen. He got some folks to listen and to begin thinking bigger. He was a poet with a rather saddened disposition, and his name was Dante Alighieri. He ultimately wrote a 14,000-line poem that went viral 200 years later called "The Divine Comedy."

Early 1400's ~ More Leaks

The Medici lending business grew tremendously, and their family educated themselves and their future generations in literature and the fine arts. This became a primary focus for the whole family for generations to come. They began to search for new artists and they paid them handsomely to custom-create art just for them. Private art: it was no longer created for the Church alone, another new concept.

125 years earlier, the city of Florence had invested in the construction of a new Church. This Church was intended to have the biggest dome in the world which was meant to echo the hugeness of their dedication to God. But because their engineers could not solve the problem of how to construct this massive dome, there remained a large circular hollow in this giant church that loomed over the city as a 125-year symbol of embarrassment and shame. Enter Filippo Brunelleschi who claimed to possess the knowledge that would complete the dome and end the city's shame. Using his self-taught knowledge of the complex architectural techniques used by the ancients, Brunelleschi successfully completed the dome, changing the fields of architecture and engineering forever.

A Papal Secretary, Poggio Bracciolini, would spend his 'vacation' time riding a mule through the hillsides of Western Europe. He was searching for documents that the ancient Greeks and Romans hid in monasteries when the Roman Empire began to fall. These docs explained the ways of life over 1,000 years before Poggio. This effort grew the collection of ancient books and knowledge about the ancients, pushing their humanistic ideals to the forefront of everyday consciousness.

A fad for educated teenaged boys was to sneak out of the walls and hitch a ride to a bigger city like Rome or Naples to rob their graveyards. They were less interested in stealing jewelry or other valuable items; they were more interested in learning the secrets of the fabled ancient Greeks & the Roman Empirical cultures.

Mid-1400's ~ The Gusher
The Florence-based Medici bank became the biggest bank in Italy paving the way for the family to attain high status as civic leaders in Florence.

The Medici family created schools where accomplished and famous maestro artists could apprentice the very best young art students, who would then supply the burgeoning art market with an increasing quantity of artists and art - all at the highest level of excellence. If you wanted to appear to possess wealth or power at this point, hiring yourself a maestro-trained artist to create personal art just for you, was the 'in' thing to do. This attracted the highest grade of young artistic talent from all around the Western world.

Mid-late 1400's ~ Concurrent Shift to the Past and the Future

This map of Florence today outlines the wall around the city as it was during the high Renaissance period.

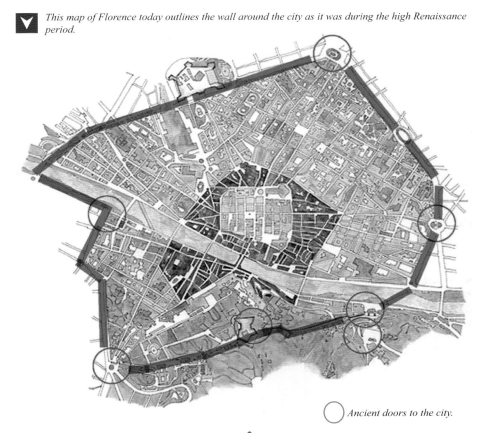

◯ *Ancient doors to the city.*

BACKGROUND

The exploding art market transitioned into several directions at once. Wealthy patrons began to prefer ancient art rather than newly-created art. Some patrons even preferred art that was themed not around the traditional religion-based stories, but shockingly around real people and real life stories.

The sciences became something that artists wanted to explore so that they could understand

> Since it was dangerous to speak one's mind, art became the expressive, and deafening 'voice' of Humanism that ultimately drowned out the Dark Ages.

how to create art that appeared to be more realistic: Guys like da Vinci and Michelangelo studied cadavers to understand what occurs beneath the skin, maximizing their ability to paint and to sculpt more realistically. Architects needed to possess a better understanding of mathematics in order to master the complex world of engineering that was needed to in order to design the beautiful buildings that the city and the patrons were now demanding in prodigious numbers.

Early-Mid 1500's ~ the Broad Brush of Humanism

The Medici bank had become the largest bank in the western world. They were the most important patrons of the arts, and they single-handedly drove the international demand for art skyward.

Gutenberg had invented the printing press in the mid-1400's. Books and pamphlets were now appearing en masse, and people began to learn to read. Reading introduced new ideas that penetrated every level of consciousness and at every income level in the land.

This movement of art, science and human expression spread wider and deeper: In Poland, a gentleman named Copernicus was decoding our position in the universe. At sea Vespucci and Columbus were discovering new worlds while Thomas More was philosophizing about humanism in England, and so forth. After 200 years, humanism had taken a firm hold.

The sheer strength of humanism was enough to catapult all of Europe out from the dismal Middle Ages and into an age of curiosity and enlightenment, rebirth and openly expressed beauty that Giorgio Vasari named the "Renaissance ."

And Florence?

For a couple of centuries, Florence basked in the glory of becoming the most important city in western Europe, and it enjoyed the reputation of being 'in style' and 'cool' in every possible way.

P.S. Although the 'High' Renaissance period lasted approximately 120 years, from the year 1400 until the death of Raphael in 1520, the entire European Renaissance period lasted nearly eight more decades until just before the 1600's. At that point, the new "Baroque" era gushed forth to dictate the styles of preferred art, fashion, music - and thinking. But that of course, is a whole other story.

BACKGROUND

Today, the streets of the Florence Historical District look quite similar to the way they might have looked 600 years ago.

TRIGGERS

A multitude of events (triggers) had to have collided in painstaking perfection in order for the Renaissance to occur. Speculation about these triggers has been highly debated for centuries. Here is a summary of those events.

BACKGROUND

BACKGROUND

The collision of events that meshed together over the period of 200 years made it possible for the Renaissance to occur.

Onset of the "Humanist" Movement	ART became the "Voice" of Humanism	Church Weakens
• The Black Plague thinned the population significantly • "Book Hunters" began to find books from the ancient Romans & Greeks • Dante: "Free Thinking" "Think for Yourself!" "YOU are important!" • Petrarch: "Remember Lucretius" "We want Science, Math & Literature!" "More Free Thinking!" • The 'voice' grows through art: The flat Byzantine style of religious art began to be over-shadowed by 'shading' created depth & perspetive - a new form of artistic realism	• Depth & Perspective advanced into more realistic styles • The new styles advanced into experiments with non-religious themes: real people, nature, real-life scenes • Nude Art was popularized • Newly-discovered Engineering techniques broadened the styles of Architecture; more refined buildings popped up • Demands to apply newer engineering techniques to military and civic functions increased • Curiosity led to exploration in the Sciences • Science strengthened to challenge religion • The Printing Press was invented; Literacy broadened knowledge • New ideas, spread like wildfire • Explorers discovered new lands and new ideas around the globe	On-going internal 'issues' plagued the Papacy: • **Papal Schism** Several 'Popes' claimed the Papacy at the same • The Papal Seat was moved from France back to Rome • The Medici became more powerful than the Church in Florence and spreading • The Monk Savonarola was executed in Florence by Papal order • Pope Leo X Bankrupted the Vatican • 'Humanism' was undermining the Church's strength • The Church shows opposition to Humanism

Throughout all of the above, something else was growing behind the scenes:
- Giovanni de'Medici became popular by lending money to the 'common' people
- Cosimo the Elder de'Medici grew the bank to become the biggest in the local City States
- Lorenzo 'the Magnificent' de'Medici grew the bank to the biggest in the entire Western World
- A HUGE amount of Wealth was used to find & fund new artists, and to build Schools where young new artists could be taught by the Grand Masters
- Cosimo I de'Medici Conquers Sienna, Lucca and other Cities to grow his Tuscan area of Rule.

The HOUSE of MEDICI grew to become the POWER behind the "Voice," and the Renaissance was that "Voice."

Palazzo Medici Riccardi
This house was designed for Cosimo (the Elder) de'Medici in 1444 by Michelozzo, whose work was greatly influenced by Brunelleschi.

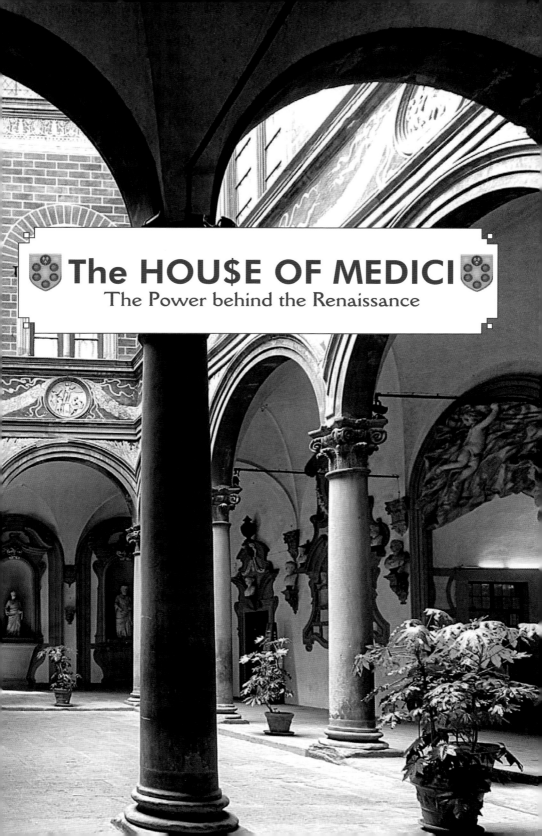

The HOU$E OF MEDICI

The Power behind the Renaissance

GIOVANNI DE' MEDICI
1360 - 1429

- Lent money to the lower classes
- Supported the 'Pirate Pope'
- Protected the interests of the common people
- Yearned to boost the family's social status

Once upon a time...

during the late Dark Ages, there lived a young man named Giovanni di Bicci de' Medici, (pronounced jo-VAHN-ee dee-BEE-chee day MED-i-chee) who worked in his father Viero's tiny little lending service in the city of Florence. This service was run in conjunction with the family's wool shop, and at that time, there were many loan services scattered throughout the land. Anyone that had possessed two florins to rub together knew that the road to wealth lay in the money-lending business. Commonly, lenders delighted in their own abilities to discover ways to cheat their clients out of a few extra percentage points upon payback. What differentiated the Medici lending service from others was that they strictly followed rules of integrity, they loaned money to the lower classes (instead of only to the wealthy) and their clients had to 'qualify' for a loan. Because Viero practiced a strict

Bust of Giovanni de' Medici by Romeo Pazzini; Museo della città di Rimini

sense of loyalty to his paying clientele, they in return remembered him when they grew to various positions of power.

Because of their fast-growing and loyal customer base, the Medici quickly grew into their own position of power among the large numbers of the lower class - or the "popolo minuto." Florence at this time was split into two factions: the upper class headed by the Albizzi family; and the 'other' class loosely led by the Medici. Viero taught his son the importance of supporting these people of the 'lower brackets,' an attitude that contributed significantly to the growth, overwhelming popularity and ultimate success of the Medici for centuries to come. Giovanni worked alongside his father Viero until he took over the business completely when Viero passed away.

From this vantage point, it is easy to see how the city of Florence may have looked during the Renaissance period.

As the winds of power changed direction in Florence, new banners (gonfalones) flew to represent a new age. During this time in Florence, wealth was synonymous with political power. Because of his already established financial success, Giovanni was given the highest-ranking civil position that any Medici held for the next 100 years. Unlike many of the future Medici who preferred to rule from less visible positions, Giovanni became the publicly known "gonfaliere" (carrier of the banner, similar to our mayor) in 1421.

The Medici family possessed an insatiable appetite for the arts and sciences. One by one, they sent their children to the available art schools to learn the fine arts of painting, sculpting and goldsmithing. When they grew up, their keen eye and formal education made them exceptionally qualified to spot talent. And so from the darkness, they recognized and sponsored new artists, like the artist of infinite fame, Donatello, whose art contributed greatly to the beginnings of the Renaissance Era.

Their money-is-no-object support of the arts led to an entirely new genre of artists that drew and painted according to what they saw in nature, rather than what was merely imagined for the church.

But still Giovanni felt a strong pull to boost the Medici social status in order to be taken more seriously within the elite strata of Florence. He wanted to embark on a project that would act as a good training ground for his son Cosimo, one where they could work together side by side as a father and son team, and one that would simultaneously boost a cohesive family image. And he found one. The issue that represented a sensitive point of shame and embarrassment for Florentines for over 125 years was the domeless Cathedral of Santa Maria del Fiore.

The Medici Family Name

Way back during the dark ages, a peasant sheep-herding family lived in the rural township of Cafaggiolo, in Tuscany. Although it has been difficult to document, stories are told that some members of this early family possessed acute medical knowledge and skills. Their fellow townspeople would often visit this family with the hopes of finding cures for ailments, diseases, injuries, and such. The family eventually hung a plaque over their door identifying themselves as Doctors (Medics), or in Italian, "Médici."

The Pirate Pope

Once upon an afternoon during the dismally Dark Ages, in the tiny walled-in town of Florence, two guys sat in a tavern slugging down their tankards of ale. Their names were Giovanni de' Medici and Baldassarre Cossa. Cossa was an honest-to-goodness pirate who had recently found himself in Florence, where he befriended Medici, the wealthy owner of the fast-growing Medici bank.

On this particular afternoon, Medici asked of Cossa "What would you like to be when you grow up?"

Gnawing thoughtfully on his half-eaten drumstick, Cossa, full-mouthed, spewed "I would like to work at the Vatican."

"Oh really?" chuckled the affable Medici.

"Yeah," continued Cossa, "but not just in ANY position. I want to be Pope, and I want YOU to give me the money I will need to make that happen!"

After a hardy round of thigh-smacking laughter, Medici straightened up and said, "OK, my friend. I'll put up the money. But when you become Pope, you had better not forget who got you there." So they banged their tankards together and shook on it.

The years passed, and Cossa had advanced quickly through the ranks to the exalted position of cardinal.

One night, Cossa invited the current pope (Alexander V) over for dinner. The funny thing, however, was that the pope returned the next day, dead. Cossa quickly took advantage of the sudden space at the top of the papal heap and claimed the papacy for himself as Pope John XXIII.

Remembering his old Medici friend, our new pope granted all of the Vatican's loans to the Medici bank. This resulted in catapulting the Medici bank - and its family - to the top of the Florentine social heap, where Giovanni de' Medici became known as "God's Banker."

P.S. After several years and a tumultuous career, Pope John XXIII was defrocked, publicly humiliated, and imprisoned for corruption and fornication (over 40 counts!). At that point, it became necessary once again for Cosimo to pull out his checkbook to bail Cossa out of jail.

A few short months later, after Cossa's death, Medici doled out yet another pouch of gold florins to pay Donatello and Michelozzo to sculpt a more-than-adequately ornate tomb for the 'Pirate Pope.'

Today, the tomb of our 'Pirate Pope' can be found in the city of Florence in the octagonal Baptistery of San Giovanni.

The end.

Epilogue

The Medici family eventually created a few popes from their own bloodline:

- (a later) Giovanni de' Medici became Pope Leo X in 1513
- Giulio di Giuliano de' Medici became Pope Clement VII in 1523
- Giovanni Angelo Medici became Pope Pius IV in 1559
- Alessandro Ottaviano de' Medici became Pope Leo XI in 1605

...and the Vatican has never been the same since.

Giovanni realized that in order to solve the problem of the cathedral, they must seek resources from other than their own traditional pool - possibly even someone who was studied in the advanced ways of ancient Rome. This was the magical answer that saved the face of the city.

And lo, the Family Medici was raised higher in social and political status than they had hoped.

Unbeknownst to anyone at that time, the Medici family money was to grow into the strongest financial and social forces that buttressed the upcoming new age later known as "The Renaissance Era."

We Must be Doing Something Right... so Let Us Celebrate!

At least this was the thinking during the first decades of the 1400's. Living in a republic, the citizens of Florence could vote on a variety of aspects of their lives. In a republic, all you had to do to deserve a vote was to belong to one of the many professional guilds and, of course, you had to be a man. The representatives of the guilds vied among each other to gain the high-guild-on-the-totem-pole status, much as they do today.

Outside Florence, other city-states saw this type of governing as a weakness so spotting this vulnerability, they sent their own leaders to try to take control of Florence. Early in the 1400's, the Duke of Milan attacked unsuccessfully because he fell ill and died before the war was over. And so the people of Florence celebrated.

A few years later, the King of Naples decided to give it a go. However, he too died before overpowering Florence. Once again, the Florentines took to the streets to celebrate their continued freedom. Then the new Duke of Milan decided to finish what his father had begun two decades earlier. The Florentines fought hard to maintain their liberties, and managed once again to eschew a take-over. And of course they celebrated, yet again.

All of that happened during the first 25 years of the 1400's. Meanwhile in the background during those same years, the city dealt with its everyday skirmishes on a local level: the wealthy Albizzi and the Strozzi families vied with each other for the top ruling positions in the city; mounting political pressures from the large population of Medici fans were pelting the Albizzi and the Strozzi like a barrage of stones from a line-up of siege cannons; Brunelleschi had successfully completed the construction of the Duomo; Donatello was decorating the city with beautiful

sculptures, and humanism was beginning to gain a firm grasp that would change the psyche of Florentines forever.

Because of the Medici success at navigating the battle-fraught waters of civic leadership, they were cast into a seemingly permanent position of a ruling power.

The people of Florence had so many reasons to celebrate, and celebrate they did.

Giovanni died in 1429, but not before successfully establishing the Medici family solidly into the hearts of the Florentine people forever.

Well, not quite.

GIANTS ~ THE PEOPLE

COSIMO DE' MEDICI
1389 - 1464

- Shy and unassuming
- Grew the Medici bank to be the biggest in Tuscany
- Took care of the under-privileged
- **Became known as Cosimo the Elder**
- **"Pater Patriae" - Father of our Country**

The Medici family enjoyed a life of wealth and power, thanks to Giovanni's good head for business and politics. The family rubbed elbows with the existing Florentine city big-wigs, while maintaining continued support of the lower classes by providing loans to those who could not get money from the more traditional banks.

Having inherited a love for the ancient arts and sciences from his father Giovanni, young Cosimo was meanwhile getting his kicks from robbing old tombs and ancient sites with his friends. 'Tomb Raiding' was a fun activity that included the cool edge of danger. They were not

Cosimo (the Elder)
de' Medici by Bronzino

looking for jewels, or pottery or even dead bodies - they were hunting for ancient documents. They were seeking clues to the 'legendary' ancient cultures that were fabled to have lived many centuries before and that ruled the world. It was widely believed that the ancients (the Greeks, the Roman and Egyptian Empires) knew things that had long since been forgotten, things that related to science, mathematics, art, engineering, literature, and philosophy. And because he grew up in a walled-in, closed-minded town, young Cosimo wanted to know more about the forward-thinking secrets from way back then. In addition, Cosimo attended his studies in art and literature, all-the-while working side by side with his father Giovanni astutely learning the ins and outs of the banking business.

Possessing a similar disposition as his father, Cosimo easily adopted Giovanni's strong morals, honesty in business and heart for those who were less fortunate than he.

Unlike his father Giovanni, Cosimo preferred to live outside of the spotlight. He shunned participation in the day-to-day issues of politics by moving to a farm in outer Tuscany. It was from there that he refined the family's lending business by loaning money to a wider area of lower class folks all throughout Tuscany who could not get money through the traditional methods in Florence, such as the majority of banks, which only toiled in servitude to the upper echelon. His loyalty to these 'outer' classes brought Cosimo to altogether new heights of respect, popularity and ultimately power among their growing numbers.

As Cosimo grew up, the political scenery in Florence wobbled back and forth between a variety of wealthy power mongers. One such family, the Albizzi (pron al-BEET-see) clan, enjoyed both prestige and power over the city for a short period of time. The Albizzi experienced a constant struggle from other 'wanna-be' high class rulers such as the Strozzi (pron STROT-zee) family, but felt a greater on-going and gnawing threat from the growth of the lower classes - led in large part by the now adult and shrewd Cosimo de' Medici and the 'outers' - and took actions to put them back into their lower places.

Early in the rise of Cosimo's power in Florence, he felt the pressure from the Albizzi to keep him and his 'lowers' in line. Fearing the worse, Cosimo moved his money out of the city where it couldn't be found. Soon, the Albizzi had Cosimo arrested and taken to a cell high in the tower of what is now called the Palazzo Vecchio.

Cosimo's right-hand guy was also arrested and tortured into giving up some secrets about his longtime friend. Cosimo himself was accused of treason and found guilty, the penalty being death. But being a republic, the Albizzi could not actually carry out the sentence without consulting the people of Florence to attain enough supporting votes, and they were making it difficult for the leaders to carry out the death sentence on Medici. On September 8, 1433 the Albizzi settled for the exile of Cosimo from Florence.

Cosimo died in Florence, and was buried in the Medici Chapel. The Chapel, designed by Filippo Brunelleschi, is located inside the Basilica di San Lorenzo.

The Gold Florin was produced from 1232 to 1533 without much alteration. One side shows the Florentine Fleur-de-Lis; on the other side, John the Baptist is standing raising his hand in benediction, and holding a cross-tipped sceptre.

It was a good thing that Cosimo had previously moved his money, ergo his banking business, out of the city before he was arrested. When he was exiled, his funds accompanied him into banishment as well. With the largest chunk of cash no longer available to the city, the Florentine officials suffered serious financial loss. In addition, great numbers of the local population fled the city to show their support for Medici. They grew tired of the problems that had befallen them since they ousted their beloved Cosimo. So, assisted by the Medici-friendly Papacy, they took over the city and sent troops to find Cosimo and beg him to return to Florence.

On the way back to Florence, Cosimo was escorted by 340 soldiers to the city of Lucca. The people of that town cheered for him for hours. The crowds lined the road from Lucca to Florence happily awaiting his return. But Florence's officials, afraid of a set-up, asked Medici to return under the cover of darkness, and to take a back road into the city and enter through a back gate. The next morning, Cosimo arose early to pay a visit to the pope (who was still in town) to thank him for assisting in bringing him home. He then walked toward his office at the Palazzo Vecchio where throngs of citizens cheered and waved banners as he quietly made his way back to work. The day was September 8, 1434 - exactly one year to the day after his exile.

With the beaten Albizzi faction now in the background, the city gave Cosimo an important seat of government. In the mean time, he reestablished his banking business in Florence, and set about to continue lending money to the underprivileged who were sadly affected by his exile. This swelled his popularity to unheard of new heights. Loyalists to the Medici bloomed in numbers so vast that even the leaders in faraway Rome and the Vatican grew in awe as they too were appropriately impressed.

GIANTS ~ THE PEOPLE

THE RISE OF THE HOUSE OF MEDICI

Unlike previous Florentine rulers such as the Strozzi and the Albizzi families, Cosimo was not known to spend lavishly on himself. He saved his considerable wealth to appease his life-long love of the arts. Scrupulously following his father's advise to stay out of the public eye, it was important to him that he did not garner envy, as this was an emotion that can cause wars. Living in a small house in a modest neighborhood, Cosimo dressed in modest clothing and he rode a mule to work every day.

Knowing in his heart that his beloved city of Florence would benefit from a growing and continuous focus on the arts, he thus found a place where his fortunes could and should be spent. He purchased great works of art for both the city and for his family. He had numerous public libraries and buildings designed and built. His friend Vespasiano da Bisticci stated in his biography of the Medici that Cosimo would often say that "Before fifty years have passed, we shall be expelled, but my buildings will remain." And although he did spend lavishly on the city, he still lived as modestly as a local merchant.

> Cosimo:
> A razor-sharp blade in a satin scabbard.

Being a man of smart money, Cosimo was known to invest in many civic projects. These projects kept people in jobs which continued the growth of money through the merchants and through the city itself. The economy was thriving and the people were beginning to feel 'comfortable' for the first time in their lives. The single most important project in Florence at this point was the building of the dome on top of the Church

> "Along with politics come the entrails of Power. It is often said that the more money you have, the more enemies you acquire. "
> ~ Niccolò Machiavelli

of Santa Maria del Fiore, which was started by his father, of which the Medici family were major financial sponsors. So many people were critical about its potential outcome that Cosimo gnashed his teeth each day as the painstakingly slow progress on the dome continued until its glorious and successful completion in 1436.

As a patron of the arts he became even more loved by the popolo (citizens) who were still strongly supported by his bank. His contributions to the city created a beautification that sent rumors to other

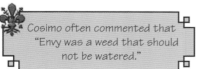

> Cosimo often commented that "Envy was a weed that should not be watered."

cities throughout Europe including Paris and Rome, who were until then considered to be the big purveyors of the arts. This in turn attracted artists from all over Europe to come to Florence where they held high hopes of finding new work.

Because of the attention garnered from the other large cities, Florence rose in popularity to become 'the cool place to be' at that time. Other wealthy Florentine families, in their desire to share in this 'spotlight of cool' also began to spend lavishly on paintings, sculptures and on the artists themselves as well. This snowball effect launched Florence into a global arena that considered it to be the most favored city in the world of art and of sophistication.

In the mean time, this fame and glory had paved the way for the Medici bank to grow exponentially and eventually to become the largest bank, and certainly the most profitable business in all of Europe. Cosimo had managed to secure a position in history for himself and for the family Medici.

Upon his death in 1464, his son Piero was thrust into the spotlight for five short years. Inheriting a solid disposition of integrity and the family love of the arts from his father and grandfather, Piero maintained the popularity and the stature of the Medici family. He had two children, Lorenzo and Giuliano. As his father did for him, Piero groomed his own shy young son Lorenzo to continue the family business, to hold the respect of those in need, and to nurture a deep love for the arts.

And it was young Lorenzo who took power five years later in 1469. **Magnificently!**

Broken Plans

Cosimo wished to rebuild the Church of San Marco, so he called his now famous architect Filippo Brunelleschi (the 'Dome' guy) to create a new model for the Church. But Filippo's plans were too ornate for Cosimo's taste, so he hired the architect Michelozzo instead. This so infuriated Brunelleschi that, in an angry huff, he smashed his own model into a thousand pieces and stormed out.

Love Me, or Leave Me

Cosimo was a clever man who ruled by clever means. On the outside he won the hearts of the Florentine citizens with his on-going beautification of their city, which gave them eternal bragging rights. However, on the inside, he was known to be (from our modern-day perspective) rather unscrupulous. For example, if a person publicly opposed him or his political views, that person was expelled to live his days outside the city walls. There, he might find robbers, pirates, thieves, rapists, or murderers. The thought of expulsion was revolting, even to the stoutest of heart.

PATER PATRIAE

Meaning "Father of the Country," Pater Patriae was a nickname given to Cosimo by the Florentine citizens upon his death. They wished it to be known that it was Cosimo de' Medici that saved their lives, fought for their honor, and made their beloved city of Florence one of the most important cities in all of Europe.

LORENZO DE' MEDICI

1449 - 1492

- Grew the Medici bank to be the largest in all of Europe
- Amassed the biggest collection of ancient books
- Patronized the arts with wide-spread social effect
- His benevolence earned him the nickname 'il Magnifico'

The Medici family held power in Florence intermittently for over 300 years, from the late 1300's to the 1700's. Having what was considered to be the largest bank in Europe definitely helped.

Lorenzo's grandfather Cosimo [the Elder] had amassed quite a fortune in land and farming that he turned into loans, thus beginning a long legacy of financial control over the community.

Lorenzo was a quiet boy who enjoyed art and poetry in addition to his outdoor interests of jousting, hunting, and birding. When his father Piero died after a brief five-year Florentine rule, Lorenzo was thrust into the political limelight, not of his own choosing.

Bust of Lorenzo (copy)
by Andrea del Verrocchio

> Although Lorenzo was a dedicated husband to his wife Clarice Orsini, he had fallen in love as a young lad, with Lucrezia Donati. He was not allowed to marry her because her family did not possess a high status, like Clarice's. But for many years to come, he wrote love poems dedicated to Lucrezia.

1469 was an important year for Lorenzo, punctuated by both love and loss. During that year, he married Clarice Orsini (of the Orsini lineage of popes). In that same year his beloved father Piero, riddled with gout, passed away. In addition, Lorenzo was handed the 'reins' of the city, much to his immediate chagrin. For, like his forebear Giovanni, Lorenzo was a quiet man who preferred to govern from the background.

During his tenure as the ruler of Florence, Lorenzo expanded his interest in the arts by focusing his keen eye (not to mention his even keener bank account) on discovering new talent. Lorenzo had a tremendous respect for the arts and sciences that included sculpture, painting, mathematics, poetry, literature and architecture. He sought out and invested in many artists whose names and works still remain important today. These would include Leonardo da Vinci, Botticelli, Verrocchio and, of course, the enigmatic Michelangelo, in addition to many more sculptors, painters, writers and poets and architects.

Like his father and grandfather before him, Lorenzo believed that people are more productive when happy, and maintaining this philosophy helped Lorenzo keep the precarious balance of peace throughout most of his tenure. This benevolence earned him the nickname of "il Magnifico."

Lorenzo, a passionate humanist, believed that people should be encouraged to expose the most favorable side of themselves. He spent his quiet hours pouring deeply over the writings of the ancient

Poet ◆ Scholar ◆ Humanist
Art Aficionado ◆ Ruler ◆ Businessman

Roman philosophers in search of ways to improve the way people perceived themselves. Cherishing the idea of open thinking, he became a centerpiece among elite scholars as they attempted to reconcile the writings of the ancients with their own modern-day social issues.

The explosion of art that occurred as a result of the Medici patronage created a sense of self-expression that had not existed for 1,000 years. This self-expression caught on quickly and contributed largely to the pulling of Florence ~ and ultimately much of Europe ~ out of the Dark Ages and into the period that we now know as the Renaissance era.

Bustling Household

Lorenzo adored seeing children scurrying all around him. His wife Clarice Orsini bore him ten children, three of whom died during birth or infancy. His son Giovanni grew up to become Pope Leo X who was of great assistance to the Medici family and their relationships within the Vatican. His son Piero (who later became known as "Piero the Unfortunate") grew up to squander the family fortune and run their business into the ground. Lorenzo adopted his nephew Giulio, who grew up to serve in the Vatican as Pope Clement VII.

If that was not enough, Lorenzo 'adopted' a couple of young artists, one of whom went by the name of Michelangelo Buonarroti. Lorenzo brought the young Michelangelo into his home to be raised alongside Medici's own children.

Together, Lorenzo and Clarice bore ten children before she died at the young age of 34 of tuberculosis. Like his own father, Lorenzo suffered from gout. And while Christopher Columbus sailed the ocean blue in 1492, Lorenzo died peacefully in his sleep. He is entombed next to his brother Giuliano in the Medici Chapel.

Upon Lorenzo's death in 1492, a few "odd duck" Medici attempted to rule the Florentines but only managed to nearly run the family 'business' into the ground. Only when Cosimo I de' Medici, the Grand Duke of Tuscany took power in 1537 did the House of Medici once again rise to a position of royal status and leadership in not just Florence this time, but in all of the increasingly important areas of Tuscany. ❧

The Tomb of Lorenzo de' Medici can be found in the Capella di Medici inside of the Basilica di San Lorenzo. It was created lovingly by Michelangelo for his patron and friend. The two sculptures in front represent Dawn and Dusk, forever under the watchful eyes of Lorenzo.

THE PEOPLE ~ GIANTS

GIANTS ~ THE PEOPLE

THE PAZZI CONSPIRACY

A somewhat quiet man, like his grand and great grandfather before him, Lorenzo preferred to rule from the background rather than the foreground. He had representatives in the city council who operated the city by means of blackmail, threats, exiles and politically-enhancing marriages. Of course this methodology fostered a bitter resentment among some members of the wealthy class who felt that they should be ones with the power to dole out these harsh punitive measures, rather than Lorenzo. One such family was the Pazzi clan.

Teaming up with the Archbishop of Pisa, who at that time was backed by the pope (Sixtus IV), they planned a conspiracy against the Medici that remains infamous to this day: One Easter Sunday while attending Mass with his younger and more handsome dear brother Giuliano, they were attacked. Giuliano was killed and Lorenzo suffered a stab wound. The citizens, recoiling at this abuse of their beloved Medici rulers, banded behind Lorenzo and sent a posse to kill the participating members of the Pazzi family, and to lynch the Archbishop of Pisa.

This angered the pope who retaliated by seizing the Medici assets, and excommunicating the ruling government of Florence. He also incited an invasion of Florence by the Duke of Calabria that cast the city into a brutal battle. Lorenzo tried to muster help from his friends in Milan, but they were busy handling their own issues with the Strozzi family and were of little assistance. So Lorenzo mounted his horse and galloped to Naples where he successfully negotiated peace with King Ferdinand of Naples. Peace reigned once again, and the citizens of Florence rallied around Lorenzo, giving him the nickname of Lorenzo "il Magnifico", the Magnificent.

The delicate balance of peace was kept (by and large) for many years to come. Until a couple of years before Lorenzo's death, a Dominican Friar by the name of Girolomo Savonarola rode into town shouting in his fire-and-brimstone manner that the city of Florence had sunk into the pits of hell with their free-thinking ways, their nude art all over the city, and their focus on money and possessions. He garnered support from many Florentines through guilt and threats of an eternity in hell which made tumultuous the last days of Lorenzo's rule.

Damned If You Do...

Upon his deathbed, Lorenzo pondered his right to ascension into the forever after. He wondered if perhaps there was some merit to the rantings of the zealot Monk Girolamo Savonarola, and whether maybe, some of his ruling methodology might not be considered to be 'heavenly' behavior. Concerned for the safety of his soul, he sent for Savonarola to come to his bedside. After hearing Lorenzo's heartfelt confessions, Savonarola scoffed and damned Lorenzo to hell. Lorenzo passed away soon after.

[This story is commonly told today by some local Florentines. Although Vasari makes mention of it in his book "Lives of the Artists," modern historians have largely disproved it. None-the-less, the story continues to live on.]

Adoption of a Young Michelangelo

Lorenzo, being educated in the arts, created a studio of sorts in a garden very near to the Basilica di Santa Croce. This is where young new talent could be honed and perfected by existing greats like maestro Masaccio.

One afternoon, as Lorenzo strolled casually through the studio, he noticed a scrap of paper balled up on the floor. He picked it up and was taken aback at the perfection of the sketch that had been so artfully drawn. When he asked who had created this sketch, Masaccio took him to meet a new teen-aged student named Michelangelo Buonarroti. At that moment, this young Michelangelo was sculpting a faun, and Lorenzo chuckled saying "Fauns are supposed to be old men with only a few rotten teeth left in their mouth. Your faun still has all of his teeth!" As soon as he went away, the boy, eager to please his patron, took a hammer and proceeded to knock out the teeth of his faun.

Lorenzo kept a watchful eye on the boy, and noting the crystal clear vision and the magnitude of sheer raw talent that the boy possessed, Lorenzo paid Michelangelo's father a handsome stipend for permission to raise the boy in the Medici household.

Finding Lorenzo Today

Lorenzo de' Medici is easily spotted within the hearts and souls of today's Florentines. But if you want more, you simply need to look around at the plethora of art and architecture around this magnificent city because Lorenzo, even though he himself was not an artist, paid for the creation of some of the most magnificent art and architecture in history.

The Church of San Lorenzo (no, it was not named after him, but for the real Saint Lawrence), has become the de facto official church of the Medici family. Inside you will find tombs and crypts for Lorenzo, Giuliano, Cosimo (the Elder), Cosimo I, Giovanni, Piero and a whole host of other Medici.

The Laurentian Library was designed by Michelangelo for his beloved patrion Lorenzo de' Medici. Lorenzo was single-handedly responsible for the burgeoning amounts of ancient books and manuscripts found here.

The Palazzo Medici Riccardi in Florence was the home of the Medici from Cosimo the Elder to Cosimo I over 100 years later

All over the city you will find the Medici coat of arms. Although each Medici had the crest customized for himself, they all contained the five balls plus the 6th ball containing the French fleur-de-lis. How many can you find as you walk through the city?

Lorenzo was a master collector of both ancient art as well as the modern art from his modern time. The vast collection of Medici art and treasure was left to the city of Florence by the last of the Medici, Anna Maria Luisa de' Medici. To commemorate this timeless gift, all of the City Museums of Florence offer free admittance each year on February 18.

THE PEOPLE ~ GIANTS

COSIMO I DE' MEDICI
1519-1574

- Returned the Medici family to a position of great power
- Gave himself the title of "Grand Duke of Tuscany"
- Upgraded the city with new schools & buildings

Cosimo I was a refined gentleman and a ruthless politician. Like his great uncle Lorenzo, he too enjoyed a passion for the arts & sciences. After a 40-year period with a variety of wanna-be leaders, Cosimo I brought back the Medici name and stature. The city had once again realized a position of not only cultural growth, but of military might as well. He decided to call himself Cosimo "I", and to avoid confusion with his forbearer, he officially gave him the posthumous title of Cosimo il Vecchio, or **Cosimo "the Elder."** He also gave himself the title of Grand Duke of Tuscany (not just of Florence, mind you), and he set about to make decisions that would significantly influence the stature ~ and size ~ of Tuscany and to ensure that echo of the Medici legends into the future.

He hired his friend and favorite architect **Giorgio Vasari** to design and build the new offices for the ruling elite. He also asked one of his favored artists and architects, Buontalenti to also contribute to its construction that concluded in 1581. Called the Uffizi (the offices), this U-shaped building sits comfortably on the bank of the Arno River and provided the massive upgrade needed to run the city. He joined the Administrative Offices, the Tribunal, and the State Archives into a single location streamlining the ever-present inefficiencies.

Today it is known as the **Uffizi Gallery** and it houses some of the most significant artistic works of the Renaissance period and forward. It is now considered to be one of the most visited museums in the world today.

Cosimo I de' Medici
by Agnolo Bronzino

Like his Medici forefathers, Cosimo I was a passionate patron of the arts. He and his family supported some of the most talented artists of his time including **Vasari, Giambologna, Buontalenti**, and **Cellini**, to name but a few. The hard sciences were also gaining ground at that point with **Galileo**, Cosimo's favorite scientist, leading the pack. In addition to supporting artists individually, he bolstered the learning environs for artists at large by directing Giogio Vasari to design the **Galleria dell' Accademia**. The Accademia is where accomplished artists worked, and where they shared their abilities by teaching and apprenticing new and upcoming talents. Today the Accademia is famous due mostly to its chief resident: **Michelangelo's** globally cherished statue of "**David**."

Cosimo I married the politically enhancing Eleanor of Toledo who bore him 11 children: 7 boys and four girls. It was she who exclaimed that she could not possibly raise her future royal children in the 'quaint' Medici Villa; she must have a newer larger house. Getting push-back from the busy Cosimo I, she decided to purchase the Pitti Palace (with her own money) and proceeded to transform it into the home of her dreams. Wishing for a safe place to ride and think, Cosimo I later added the **Boboli Gardens** in the backyard. It also served as a more-than-adequate backyard playground for the eleven children that he bore with Eleanor, plus the two illegitimate children he fathered with Eleanora degli Albrizzi (after his wife Eleanor's death), plus the two children he fathered with his second wife Camilla

Martelli. (He also fathered a daughter before his first marriage, but she did not grow up in the **Pitti Palace**.)

Possessing the understanding that an elite ruler must avoid the streets for fear of assassination, Cosimo I looked to **Giorgio Vasari** once again to build an overland tunnel between his home and his office **(Uffizi)**. This over-ground tunnel is known as the Vasari Corridor. In addition, Cosimo I flexed his military might by conquering Lucca and Pisa to expand his Tuscan territory. He then renewed the University of Pisa architecturally.

After Cosimo I's death in 1574, the Medici empire eroded and never managed to regain the stature that was once enjoyed by its predecessors.

The End.

Well not really. 300 years later Florence became the capital of Italy for five short years beginning in 1865. This temporary status was the shot in the arm the Florentines needed to refurbish their old city. Streets were straightened, centuries-old buildings were renovated, and old muck was cleaned up.

Today, when you walk the streets of Florence, you will see evidence of the rich Medici lives and stories everywhere you go. The Florentines are so proud of this gilded and colorful history that it shows on every street, in every piazza and in every single Florentine smile.

And of these, you will find many.

The End... really. ❧

Looking down from the top floor inside the Pitti Palace enables you to feel the grandeur for which Cosimo I de' Medici was so famous.

THE PEOPLE ~ GIANTS

GIANTS ~ THE PEOPLE

The three lilies on the top blue ball of the Medici coat of arms were put there upon the wishes of Cosimo (il Vecchio - the elder) de' Medici. The King of France, in thanks for support and assistance, gave Cosimo the honor of putting France's representational flower onto his own family's crest. They represent the three virtues that were most important to Cosimo: Temperance, Prudence and Fortitude.

A heroic tribute to Cosimo I, created by Giambologna, proudly oversees the community in the Piazza della Signoria.

Background: One of the many Medici Coats of Arms found throughout the City of Florence.

Finding the Medici Today

Medici coats of arms & crests *(right)* can be found on buildings, over doors, and other random places around the city. A smattering of sculptures that pay tribute to this historical family are ever-present as well.

Pitti Palace (Palazzo Pitti) is on the south side of the river, just one block from the Ponte Vecchio bridge.

The **Vasari Corridor** can be seen running overhead from the Pitti Palace across the Ponte Vecchio, through the Uffizi Museum and terminating at the Palazzo Vecchio.

The **Uffizi Museum** was the brain-child of Cosimo I de' Medici. Designed by Giorgio Vasari, it was to be the new offices of the city's officials.

The **Medici Chapel** (Capella de Medici) is where you will find the crypts and tombs of all of the prominent Medici family members including Giovanni, Cosimo the Elder, Lorenzo, his brother Giuliano, and Cosimo I, among others.

The **Laurentian Library**, designed by Michelangelo, was created for Lorenzo de' Medici.

Forte di Belvedere was built by Grand Duke Ferdinando I de' Medici during the period 1590–1595, with Bernardo Buontalenti as the designer.

Palazzo Riccardi Medici was designed by Michelozzo for Cosimo the Elder. It was the Medici family home until Cosimo I moved his family to the Pitti Palace nearly 200 years later.

The Accademia, where "David" lives, was designed by Giorgio Vasari for Cosimo I.

The **Church of San Marco** was rebuilt by Michelozzo for Cosimo the Elder de' Medici.

The Medici Family Coat of Arms varied in design over the centuries of Medici rule. In all cases, it presents the 6 balls - 5 red & 1 blue - against a gold shield. As you roam through the city, look at some of the taller buildings and churches and notice the proud collection of the Medici Coat of Arms near the roof-lines or over doorways. See how many different Medici Coat of Arms & Crests you can find.

Mafia Roots

The word "mafioso" originated in Sicily, and could be defined as "Swagger." More loosely defined, it can mean bravado, boldness, arrogance, or fear-invoking.

The history of the Mafia goes way back to the late 13th century when lethal raids of Sicily were commonplace. It seemed that **everyone** wanted to control this strategically located island, and so attempted to unseat the local Sicilians. "Everyone" included the Romans, the Phoenicians, the French and the Spaniards among others.

Because of predictable and ongoing violence, every single Sicilian leader feared for his own life every single day. Although not the first to do so, it has been observed that the Medici, way up north in Florence, practiced the structure of governing whereby family members were placed in the highest positions of strength around them. Trust was of the utmost priority, and because the bond within a family is the highest bond between men, a higher form of trust could not be acquired. Strict adherence to a code of secrecy and loyalty was required, with the fear of death and replacement as the motivation. Therefore, sequestering themselves behind a wall of trusted family members might have been the only way to survive their terms of leadership. If a Medici ever offered to pay you (as a trusted family member) to help with the running of affairs, it would be an offer that you couldn't refuse.

THE G⬡DFATHERS
PART 0

A modern day debate about whether the family Medici were ruthless tyrants, benevolent art lovers or the first Mafia family, has been discussed ad nauseam. Being a long-time student of archaeology and anthropology, it has been drummed into my thinking that our job is not to judge history but simply to observe. Our own standards of socially acceptable behavior have most certainly changed, and will continue to change. With this in mind, it is important to note that these may not be correct assessments.

Tyrannical Leaders?

The early Medici (Giovanni, Cosimo and Lorenzo) did not prefer the spotlight, so they managed the city from a distance. They had people that would carry out the day-to-day actions required to get what they wanted such as bribery, raids and executions, among other methods. However, in their defense, most all rulers in the Dark Ages were governed by these same tactics - including the Church - and they were considered to be within acceptable boundaries of the entire ruling classes. Although the Medici preferred to control the population from the background by remote control through their thugs, many of the other leaders/rulers preferred to dole out these punishments in person.

Benevolent Patrons of the Arts?

Of this there is no doubt. The Medici were steadfast and generous in their patronage, support and growth of the fine arts, literature and the concept of Humanism. The amount of money and resources they put toward the arts has, to this date, been unmatched. Their sponsoring of the arts gave a voice to the people that had not been enjoyed since the days of the ancient Roman Empire, over 1,000 years earlier. This voice-via-art was the main force behind the expulsion of the Middle Ages and the true definition of the rebirth of the human spirit or the Renaissance.

A Mafia Family?

The question remains: Were the Medici a Mafia family? Strictly speaking, no. The Mafioso concept originated in Sicily as a result of the constant attacks by surrounding countries. The Medici, although they lived nearly 500 miles from Sicily, had perfected the practice of placing their family members in strategic positions of power, and according to the locals, it was made perfectly clear to the inner circles (or 'cognoscenti') that they would live under a sworn oath of loyalty for fear of the unspeakable. And everyone knew that the 'unspeakable' would be performed publicly as a lesson to thwart any future disloyalties by other members of the cognoscenti.

THE MEDICI BANK
THE MONEY BEHIND THE RENAISSANCE

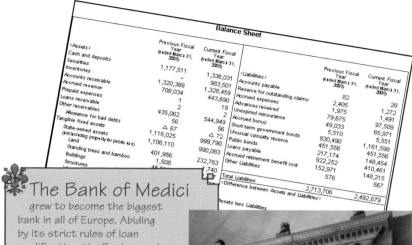

Balance Sheet		
<Assets>	Previous Fiscal Year (ended March 31, 2008)	Current Fiscal Year (ended March 31, 2009)
Cash and deposits	1,177,511	1,336,031
Securities	–	983,501
Inventories	1,320,389	1,328,459
Accounts receivable	708,034	443,690
Accrued revenue	1	19
Prepaid expenses	2	2
Loans receivable	435,062	544,949
Other receivables	56	56
Allowance for bad debts	△ 67	△ 72
Tangible fixed assets	1,116,025	999,790
State-owned assets	1,106,110	990,083
(not including property for public use)		
Land	401,956	232,763
Standing trees and bamboo	1,508	1,740
Buildings	45,91	
Structures		

<Liabilities>	Previous Fiscal Year (ended March 31, 2008)	Current Fiscal Year (ended March 31, 2009)
Accounts payable	82	28
Reserve for outstanding claims	2,405	1,272
Accrued expenses	1,975	1,491
Advances received	79,675	97,509
Unexpired reinsurance	49,033	65,971
Accrued bonus	5,510	5,551
Short-term government bonds	830,490	1,161,598
Unusual casualty reserve	451,556	451,556
Public bonds	217,174	148,454
Loans payable	922,252	410,461
Accrued retirement benefit cost	152,971	148,215
Other Liabilities	576	567
Total Liabilities	2,713,706	2,492,679
<Difference between Assets and Liabilities>		
Assets less Liabilities		

The Bank of Medici

grew to become the biggest bank in all of Europe. Abiding by its strict rules of loan qualification, the Bank was also known for its contribution to business accounting by improving the general ledger system through the development of the double-entry bookkeeping system for tracking credits and debits. This system is by and large the same system we use in accounting and bookkeeping today.

The Portal (doorway) of one of the Medici Bank branches was preserved from the 15th century and stands on display in the Museum of Ancient Art in the Sforza Castle complex in Milan.

Through the Medici leadership, Florence enjoyed an esteemed position of cultural importance through the discovery and funding of such greats as Leonardo da Vinci, Botticelli, Galileo, and of course a child artist called Michelangelo Buonarroti. Florence basked in the knowledge that their city had become the 'cool' place to be in all of Europe - if indeed you wanted to be seen as cultured and intelligent. For awhile the people enjoyed this popular status and their favorite leader became known as "Lorenzo the Magnificent" or simply "il Magnifico."

The Medici family provided the wealth and the personal support
to the artists, architects, scientists & inventors that created
so many of the lasting works that we are still familiar with today
- nearly 600 years later!

THE PEOPLE ~ GIANTS

THE PEOPLE
THE GIANTS THAT CHANGED THE WORLD
In the order of their birth

DANTE ALIGHIERI
1265 - 1321

- The Father of the Italian language
- The Thinker that formed the concepts of humanism
- The Poet that gave us our visual images of Hell
- Penned a 14,000-line poem called the "Divine Comedy"

It is known that for a period of time Dante was home-schooled and that he spent much time reading and studying poetry. During his childhood, his marriage was prearranged to Gemma di Manetti Donati. But by the time he married her, he had already fallen hopelessly in love with another young woman with whom he never had the pleasure of even a conversation: the inaccessible Beatrice. With Gemma, however, he loyally remained married and bore three children: Pietro, Jacopo and Antonia. (The exact total number of Dante's children is not really known because it was common that people would 'say' they were the children of a famous person. Without official records, these details could not be verified.)

During his life in Florence, Dante was known mainly because of his outspoken political disposition. He regularly wrote letters to the 'Powers that Be.' He attempted to mitigate a change that would free people's thinking, reminding them of the ideas that had long since been forgotten from the days of ancient Rome & Greece: "Humanism." He walked the streets of Florence happy to speak his views to whoever would listen.

During his lifetime, the political scene in Florence was turbid at best. The city was divided between those that were loyal to the Church ~ the party of the Guelphs, and those whose loyalties lay with the throne of the Holy Roman Emperor ~ the Ghibelline party. He rode during the Battle of Campaldino for the Guelph Party, whose success brought about changes in the oft-edited Constitution of Florence.

Dante Alighieri portrait by his friend Sandro Botticelli.

GIANTS ~ THE PEOPLE

Poet ◆ Philosopher ◆ Thinker ◆ Author
Humanist ◆ Father of the Italian Language

With an interest in public life, it became necessary by law for him to join one of the professional guilds in order for him to continue. So to further his interests, he joined the Physicians and Apothecaries Guild. He became involved with the city council on a variety of positions where his excellent speaking skills led him to the forefront as a communicator.

STRIPPING DANTE

With politics often comes the collision of personalities, and Dante's Guelph party became divided into two factions: the White Guelphs and the Black Guelphs. In 1301, his White Guelphs, were overtaken by the Black Guelphs who either exiled or executed members of the White Guelphs. Dante, who was visiting in Rome when this occurred, was sentenced to two years in exile from Florence (the city he loved to his very core) plus a hefty fine.

Since he could no longer legally return to Florence, he remained in Rome and fired off a seemingly unending stream of letters to Florentine officials castigating the current leadership in an effort to get people to see things differently. In addition, he refused to pay the fine saying that his actions are merely views of the mind therefore he was innocent of any crime. Florentine officials, vexed by his outpouring of opposing views, 'upped' his sentence to an eternal sentence (instead of the initial two years), stating that if he were ever to return to Florence, he would be burned at the stake.

> "Consider your origin; you were not born to live like brutes, but to follow virtue and knowledge."
> ~ Dante Alighieri

Saddened by this heartless exile, Dante roamed throughout Tuscany, all-the-while extolling the virtues of 'Free Thinking' until he ultimately landed in Bologna. After a short period, Bologna found a new relationship with Florence, and agreed to expel all Florentine exiles. Once again, Dante found himself roving the Tuscan townships of Verona and Lucca where he found many friendships. But he never found a place that made him feel as at home as did his beloved Florence. He felt stripped of all things dear to him, when they took his city and his home.

During his exile, he wrote many poems. The one that has given him a forever-after place in history was "A Divine Comedy," a detailed narrative of the path that one follows through Earth, Purgatory and ultimately, Heaven. His words were so descriptive that when it was finally published in 1555 - over 200 years after his death, Dante was exalted as the writer and poet who impacted the way people saw themselves, saw life and most importantly, how they viewed the afterlife.

Upon his death in 1321, his criminal sentence in Florence, as was commonplace in those days, was then passed down to his sons. 🌸

GIANTS ~ THE PEOPLE

ABANDON ALL HOPE YE WHO ENTER HERE.

 Dante holds a copy of his book "A Divine Comedy," next to the entrance to Hell, the seven terraces of Mount Purgatory and the city of Florence, with the spheres of Heaven above, in this fresco created by Domenico di Michelino. It is currently mounted on the wall inside of the Cathedral of Santa Maria del Fiore, under il Duomo.

THE DIVINE COMEDY

Dante's epic 14,233-line poem is divided into 3 parts in which he defines his creative vision of Heaven, Hell and Purgatory. More specifically, it describes one's journey into and through the afterlife to (hopefully) heaven.

The Poem is divided into 3 parts: Inferno, Purgatorio and Paradiso. In it, the reader is led through Dante's own journey as the Roman poet Virgil acts as his guide through Hell and Purgatory; and his 'ideal woman' Beatrice, guides him through Heaven.

The "Divine Comedy" seems to be an allegory of life and of the Florentine political arena as he saw it. Visions of Florence are illustrated in emotional detail throughout the "Hell" portion of this poetic journey.

Why is it called a "Comedy"?

In those days, there were only two general categories of literature: Tragedy (a sad ending) and Comedy (a happy ending). Tragedies were written in the formal Latin, while Comedies were written in the vernacular. Dante wanted this piece to be read and understood by the 'common man' so he wrote it in the everyday Tuscan language. Today we know this language as Italian, and henceforth, Dante has been called 'The Father of the Italian Language."

P.S. Dante originally titled the book "Comedy". Later a fellow named Boccaccio renamed it "A Divine Comedy".

Price of Fame

In those days, it was not unusual for strangers to appear in a famous person's life, claiming to be their long lost child. Since there was no real way to prove otherwise, superstars did not always know the exact number of children they were responsible.

In 2005, the City of Florence (finally) voted to exonerate Dante of his crimes and end his sentence - nearly 700 years after his death!

Dante's Eternal Love & Muse

When he was 9 years old, Dante's father took him to a family party where he first became entranced with an 8-year-old little girl named Beatrice Portinari. He was so taken with her that he could not get her out of his mind. He dreamed about her. She began to appear in his poetry. Although he would walk through the city regularly with the hopes that he might catch a glimpse of her, he saw her only one more time during her life. Beatrice married another man, Simone de' Bardi and died at the young age of 24 before Dante ever had an actual conversation with her.

Thoughts of the-Beatrice-that-could-have-been influenced Dante's thinking and ultimately his writings. She has been commonly identified as the principal inspiration for Dante's "Vita Nuova," and is also commonly identified with the Beatrice who appears as one of his guides in the Divine Comedy in the last four canti of "Purgatorio," and in the last book "Paradiso."

Although Dante married Gemma Donati and fathered three-ish children (see "Price of Fame" above), he continued to pay tribute to Beatrice for the rest of his life.

THE PEOPLE ~ GIANTS

GIANTS ~ THE PEOPLE

The Chart of Hell as depicted in this famous
painting by Sandro Botticelli.

With over 14,000 lines, **"A Divine Comedy"** is a poetic narrative about a man who, halfway through his life, realizes that he may be on the wrong path, and therefore may never make it to heaven after he departs this earth. So he hooks up with Virgil who explains that because this path is blocked by a leopard, a hungry lion and a mad she-wolf, they must proceed down a different path on their journey to eternity. On this path, he will be able to see some of the long-departed souls who have never made it past Hell. As they enter through the broad gates, he can see that there seems to be a complicated hierarchy of circles, rings and trenches. Each of these circles, rings and trenches is occupied by a different type of sinner:

Circle One - Those in limbo
Circle Two - The lustful
Circle Three - The gluttonous
Circle Four - The hoarders
Circle Five - The wrathful
Circle Six - The heretics
Circle Seven - The violent
Ring 1. Murderers, robbers, and plunderers
Ring 2. Suicides and those harmful to the world
Ring 3. Those harmful against

God, nature, and art, as well as usurers
Circle Eight - The Fraudulent
Bowge (Trench) I. Panderers and Seducers
Bowge II. Flatterers
Bowge III. Simoniacs
Bowge IV. Sorcerers
Bowge V. Barrators
Bowge VI. Hypocrites
Bowge VII. Thieves
Bowge VIII. Counselors

Bowge IX. Sowers of Discord
Bowge X. Falsifiers
Circle Nine - Traitors
Region i: Traitors to their kindred
Region ii: Traitors to their country
Region iii: Traitors to their guests
Region iv: Traitors to their lords

The man emerges from Hell on Easter Sunday and is able to see the stars in the heavens. To enjoy the complete the journey, please read "A Divine Comedy" by Dante Alighieri.

THE HOUSE WHERE DANTE LIVED

Today, the house that was once the 14th-century home of the Alighieri family is dedicated to the life and writings of this soulful man. The three-story house is divided into the three parts that represent the three most important periods in his life.

The first floor is dedicated to his childhood, home life and his days in public office. Many documents are available that speak of his Christening in the Baptistery San Giovanni in the Church of Santa Maria del Fiore. They cover his education and his election to public office. Dante's personal conflicts in office during the days of war are well documented as well.

The second floor is devoted to his exile from Florence in 1301. He travelled from town to town to find a place that he could love as much as he did his beloved city of Florence. Unable to find such a place, he settled in Ravenna where he lived for the remainder of his life.

The third floor holds many of the wonderful dedications to this lovely man. After his death, the citizens of Florence realized the huge mistake that was made in his exile, and they in turn wanted to show their loyalty and gratitude to him posthumously through their art. Included are works by such greats as Giotto, Angelico, Ghirlandaio, Raphael, Michelangelo and many others.

Before his exile from Florence, Dante would often be seen strolling through the city hoping to catch a glimpse of his beloved Beatrice. In this painting by Henry Holiday (1884), Dante stands nonchalantly on the Ponte Santa Trinità as he watches her go by. She is wearing white while strolling with two other women.

The outside wall of Dante's house toady stands as a museum dedicated to the life and writings of Dante. In it you will also enjoy a large topographical map of the city during his time, as well as explanations of technologies that were used in that period of time, such as the art of goldsmithing.

THE PEOPLE ~ GIANTS

Finding Dante Today

Throughout his life in Florence, Dante was known to stay close to home, leaving his house only to attend church in the little chapel across the street, Santa Margherita de' Cerchi. This is where you can stop in to see the tomb of Beatrice Portinari (left), Dante's lifetime love and muse. Near her tomb is a basket where visitors can leave coins accompanied by letters asking for help with their own love interests, with the hopes that Beatrice can provide solutions.

A stroll past the Uffizi Gallery will put you in the very best of company. The slightly-larger-than-life statues include Dante, Columbus, Cosimo de' Medici, Galileo and many other Giants of the Renaissance era.

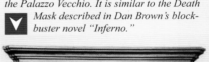

Dante's Death Mask as seen today on display in the Palazzo Vecchio. It is similar to the Death Mask described in Dan Brown's block-buster novel "Inferno."

Dante's exile from Florence required that he live henceforth anywhere other than the beloved city in which he was born. He settled in several different cities ultimately ending up in Ravenna where he died in 1321. Although his tomb is in Ravenna, this sculpture stands with grandeur outside of the Church of Santa Croce. In addition, a 'tribute' tomb can be found inside the church, appropriately included among the other Renaissance Giants.

Dante is still cherished by the Florentine people today. This fact is made clear by the sheer abundance of Dante-related places to go and things to see. In nearly every part of the city, you will find tributes to Dante expressed in endless ways.

Among the many tributes to the memory of Dante in Florence today, you will see a few modern tributes as well, such as this bust of Dante that sits on the Bar of a restaurant in Florence called (appropriately enough) Dante's Restaurant.

A DANTE ALIGHIERI
L' ITALIA
M · DCCC · LXV

THE PEOPLE ~ GIANTS

GIOTTO
1266/67 - 1337

- Father of the Renaissance
- Creator of the Campanile "Giotto's Bell Tower"
- Initiated a departure from the old Gothic art style

Giotto was born in 1266 in the little Tuscan town of Vespignano, during a time when art was not a result of independent creativity but that of the behest of the Church. His pointed departure from the traditionally accepted style of art changed western art forever and assured his place in art history for centuries to come.

Early in his career, the good-natured Giotto travelled throughout the 'boot' with his mentor and friend, the famous artist Cimabue. Cimabue's sterling reputation made it easy for him to acquire work for Giotto, thus enabling the young Giotto to gain notoriety for his own works. In Rome, he created extraordinary frescoes (paintings on wet plaster) in the Scrovegni Chapel and was hired by the Cardinal Giacomo Gaetani Stefaneschi to create pieces for (the old)St. Peter's Basilica in Rome, most notably the "Stefaneschi Triptych" which now resides in the Vatican.

Portrait of Giotto in a painting "5 Famous Men" by Uccello. This piece hangs in the Louvre.

Although he was trained in the accepted idealized and flat Byzantine style of religious art that was popular and accepted in that time, Giotto delighted in 'shading' his figures which gave them a more realistic depth and usage of space. He also enjoyed painting images that he saw in real life rather than in the traditional Biblical stories. It is because of this nearly total departure from the 'norm' that Giotto has been flagged as the **"Father of the Renaissance."** From that point forward, new and upcoming artists incorporated many of Giotto's styles into their own works, radically changing the way people viewed art forever after. This is considered by many to be the beginning of Renaissance Art.

Giotto was often seen hanging out with his closest friend **Dante Alighieri.** Dante was so taken with his work that he wrote about the artist in one of his poems, stating that "...Giotto was the artist that surpassed the elder Cimabue's abilities." Early on, Giotto had apparently liberated himself from his teacher's traditional styles and became known for his ability to imitate nature in his work.

Giotto was a man with a happy disposition, although he was also known for his unattractiveness. He was nevertheless married and bore 6 children, and provided them with a life of wealth and luxury.

He was later appointed as Magnus Magister (Great Master) and the Chief of Public Works by the city of Florence. It was in this capacity that he began his most famous project: the design and construction of the Campanile next to the Florence Baptistery. It was during this project that he died at age 71, and the project was completed by Andrea Pisano. 🌸

Painter ✦ Sculptor ✦ Architect
Father of the Renaissance

Not-so-Cheery O's

And so it is told that Pope Boniface VIII (1294) was in the market for a new painter. He had heard the rumblings that Florence was producing a 'winnowing basket' full of new artists. So he sent a courier to Florence to obtain samples from these artists. When the messenger found Giotto, he explained his assignment. Giotto did the most curious thing: he filled his brush with red paint, pinned his arm to his side (making a compass of it) and proceeded without moving his hand to draw a perfect circle. Giotto then gave this to the boy, who was convinced that he was being mocked, but he nevertheless included the red circle with the other samples that he brought back to the Pope. Whilst the Pope was looking at this curious red 'O' the courier explained how Giotto painted it without ever moving his arm and without even using a compass. The Pope, with merriment, declared that Giotto had clearly surpassed all of the other painters! Giotto was hired forthwith to create five scenes from the life of Christ in St. Peter's Basilica (it has since been redesigned, and remodeled over the centuries), which he completed with such perfection that from that point forward, never did he create a work of art that was considered to be of matching perfection. Upon seeing these five scenes, the Pope asked Giotto to decorate the whole of the interior of the chapel with scenes from both testaments.

P.S. This story of the 'O' spread throughout the land giving rise to a commonly-used saying (at that time) that referred to a stupid person: "You are rounder than Giotto's O!" *(I guess you had to be there.)*

Giotto's Portrait of his good friend Dante Alighieri

This statue of Giotto can be found in the outdoor gathering of 'Giants' in the courtyard outside of the Uffizi Gallery.

GIOTTO

GIANTS ~ THE PEOPLE

Shoo, Fly!

Locals tell the story that during his time as a student of Cimabue, Giotto mischievously painted a small housefly onto one of his paintings. When his teacher Cimabue approached and saw the very realistic-looking fly, he attempted to swat it away, causing raucous laughter from the spirited young Giotto.

Finding Giotto Today

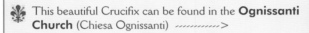

- The most visible vestige of Giotto's genius can be seen from almost anywhere along the Florentine skyline. It is **the Campanile** (Bell Tower) that stands next to il Duomo.

- This beautiful Crucifix can be found in the **Ognissanti Church** (Chiesa Ognissanti) ············>

- Within the **Uffizi Gallery** you will find Giotto's "Ognissanti Madonna." In Hall 2 you will see 3 Giotto altar pieces.

- Giotto painted fresoes in four Chapels within the church of **Santa Croce:** those of the Giugni, Tosinghi-Spinelli, Bardi, and Peruzzi families. However, the Giugni & Tosinghi-Spinelli fresoes are gone, but the Bardi & Peruzzi frescoes, although heavily restored are still there for your enjoyment.

- One of the important treasures within **Santa Maria Novella** is Giotto's exquisite crucifix. ·······>

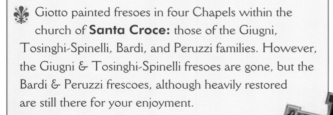

- "St. Stephen," Giotto's painting on a panel, can be found in the Museo Horne, Florence.

- The stunning altarpiece the "Baroncelli Polyptych" can be found in the Basilica of **Santa Croce.**

- The **Virtual Uffizi** website has a brief biography of Giotto: *http://www.VirtualUffizi.com/giotto.html*

NOTE: Because of the fragile nature of frescoes, many of Giotto's paintings did not survive the ravages of history. However, some of his works have been carefully preserved and can still be found in Florence today.

"When the methods and outlines
of good painting had been buried for
so many years by the ruins of war,
Giotto alone, although born among inept
artists, revived through God's grace
what had fallen into an evil state and
brought it back to such a form that it
could be called good. And it was truly
an extraordinary miracle that such an
ignorant and incompetent age could have
inspired Giotto to work so skillfully that
drawing, of which men during those times
had little or no knowledge, came fully back
to life through his efforts." ~ Giorgio
Vasari, "Lives of the Artists"

Sheep Sitting

As a little boy in a small farm town north of
Florence, Giotto spent much of his time in
the fields tending to the sheep. He would look
around, and in the dirt he would draw what
he saw in front of him.

One day a locally renowned artist named
Cimabue happened to walk by as the young
Giotto was drawing the picture of a sheep
onto a stone. Impressed with the Boy's
ingenuity, Cimabue approached Giotto's
father to gain permission to take the boy to
Florence where he could be taught to hone
his talents. This young favorite student
soon not only equaled Cimabue's skills, but
he quickly surpassed his famous teacher's
abilities.

*One of the few structures that dominates the Florentine
skyline is Giotto's Bell Tower, also known as "The
Campanile." It was designed in 1334 by Giotto who
died before the completion of the tower. It was finally
finished 25 years later in 1359 by Andrea Pisano who
remained loyal to Giotto's original design. The 16 life-
sized sculptures housed in niches around the exterior
of the tower were created by Renaissance greats
such as Donatello and della Robbia.*

GIANTS ~ THE PEOPLE

PETRARCH
1304 - 1374

- Coined the term "humanism," the philosophy that fueled the Renaissance
- Created the first and most eloquent writings on humanism
- Coined the term "Dark Ages" to define the age before his own birth

Sketch of Petrarch by Altichiero da Verona.

Born Francesco Petrarcha, he was born in the little Tuscan town known as Arezzo. His father, a lawyer, insisted that he and his brother study law, but after doing so Petrarch was known to having said that "...those seven years were wasted years." He instead wished to write lyrical poetry and philosophy - the genres in which he ultimately enjoyed wide public acclaim.

On his many jaunts, he collected ancient and decrepit documents, many of which were written by a variety of Roman and Greek philosophers. For instance, he unearthed lost writings from the ancient philosopher Cicero. In them, Petrarch learned of a world vastly different than the world he was raised in.

He learned that 1,000 years before, people had lived for themselves rather than for the Church. He learned that people could choose their education and their own direction in life. And that regular citizens had, he discovered, knowledge of things that were foreign to him: mathematics, engineering, architecture, science, philosophy, literature and self-discovery.

In 1336, accompanied by his brother, he climbed to the top of France's Mt. Ventoux, a vertical trek of over 6,200 feet. While on this mountain, he experienced an epiphanous moment in which he came to understand that the centuries before his own birth should henceforth be known as the "Dark Ages" because of the obvious squelching of the human spirit by the Church and governments. Because of his pondering of the writings of his Latin idols Seneca, Virgil and most especially Cicero, he came to see that the world into which he was currently living was one of blindness and deafness. His ascent of Mt. Ventoux, he felt, was merely an allegory of man's quest for a better life: Climbing to the top enabled him to see the light.

His fascination with the ancient philosophies kept him awake at night as he pursued answers to the myriad of questions that vexed his mind. He ultimately felt compelled to include these ancient stories and philosophies into his own visionary writings and poetry, and is known to be the first to pen his views on ancient life which he termed the "humanist" way of life.

For decades his pen fluttered in a whirlwind of Latin articulation as he extolled the virtues of humanism, a way of life that he felt should be brought into the light and practiced as the normal way of daily living. He wrote poems, verbose philosophies, and mountains of letters, many

Scholar ◆ Philosopher ◆ Writer ◆ Poet
Book Hunter ◆ Father of Humanism

of which have been lost over the centuries since. At times he discussed his unrequited (imaginary?) love for "Laura" and other times he scoffed at the constant comparisons between himself and Dante Alighieri. He wished to make it clear that his lifelong intellectual and philosophical idols were not from his own generation, but they lived over 1,000 years before.

He amassed quite a legion of dedicated followers who felt it was their mission to spread the word of 'humanism'. This movement gathered momentum and was represented by many voices. During his own lifetime he actually saw his 'humanist' views taking root in Florentine society.

The budding Renaissance was born. 🌸

Petrarch discovered the ancient writings of Cicero that caused him to start the whole ball of Humanism to roll. This changed everything.

Accidental Tourist

Known as one of the first citizens to roam about merely for pleasure rather than purpose, it is said that Petrarch became known as **the First Tourist.**

The city of Florence honors Petrarch with this "pondering" sculpture that stands among the gallery of Giants outside of the Uffizi Gallery. ▶

FRANCESCO PETRARCA

FILIPPO BRUNELLESCHI
1377 - 1446

- Monumental problem solver
- Successfully designed the biggest dome ever made
- Architectural innovator, self-taught engineering genius
- Created 'linear perspective'
- One of five 'Giants' whose work signaled massive change

Filippo, born with the untoward name of Filippo di ser Brunellesco di Lippo Lapi, was raised by his mother Giuliana Spini and his lawyer father. They gave him a literary education with the hopes that he would eventually follow in this father's lawyerly footsteps. But being artistically inclined, young Filippo joined the Silk Merchants Guild which conveniently for him, included goldsmiths, metalworkers, and bronze workers. This enabled Filippo to broaden his creative skills and to be presented with multiple opportunities (which he embraced wholeheartedly) to gain experience working with a wide variety of materials.

His first major engagement was to contribute to the design and building of the *Ospedale degli Innocenti* (Hospital of the Innocents). At age 24, he learned of an upcoming competition in his hometown of Florence to design the new doors to the Baptistery, in bronze. Filled with excitement, he fled his current commission (much to the dismay of his current employer) and headed straight for Florence where he submitted a sample of his work in bronze. But much to his own dismay, the job was lost to Ghiberti, whose work

Brunelleschi painted by Masaccio, now in the Brancacci Chapel.

was so honored that he was automatically given the commission to create the third set of doors for the Baptistery.

With broad interests in engineering, mathematics, and ancient monuments, Brunelleschi participated in a variety of projects. These included the design of the Basilica and the Sagrestia Vecchia (Old Sacristy) of San Lorenzo, the meeting hall of the Palazzo di Parte Guelfa, the Pazzi Chapel and, the Santo Spirito di Firenze. He even spent some time in the maritime world designing the ship called "Il Badalone." This vessel was designed to efficiently transport marble from Pisa and Carrera on the Arno River to Florence.

Filippo's greatest work was his relentless pursuit of the completion of il Duomo, the double-domed wonder that remains standing for you to enjoy today, 600 years later.

Brunelleschi was buried beneath Santa Maria del Fiore with a plethora of honors in the Florence Chapel with this epitaph of gratitude: "Both the magnificent dome of this famous church and many other devices invented by Filippo the architect, bear witness to his superb skill. Therefore, in tribute to his exceptional talents, a grateful country that will always remember buries him here in the soil below." 🌸

Architect ◆ Sculptor ◆ Engineer
Draftsman ◆ Mathematician ◆ Inventor

Problems Atop Problems

Around 1420, the Florence Signoria (town council), led by Giovanni de' Medici, decided to hold a contest to see who might qualify to be the best person(s) to solve the problem of the uncapped Cathedral, once and for all. The Medici, always in search of publicly visible projects to boost their political popularity, put up the money to pay for the completion of the construction of this treasured Basilica di Santa Maria del Fiore. Enter: Filippo Brunelleschi. Not only was he a talented (self-taught) architect, Brunelleschi was also quite skilled in other areas such as math and engineering. In addition, he possessed some of the architectural secrets of the ancient Romans. These skills gave him the ability to solve many problems that arose during the construction of the Duomo.

At that time, artists and architects were taught to 'see' in two dimensions. This meant that when they designed a structure, the plans were drawn up using a flat two-dimensional drawing style. And this made it difficult to design a building that was other than a basic square or rectangle. This old flat drawing style would not be helpful in creating the plans for the new Duomo. They needed the ability to visualize their sketches with depth before construction could begin. Brunelleschi, being trained to forge gold and bronze artworks in a three-dimensional space, created and perfected the art of linear perspective. This is a theory in which the relative size, shape, and position of objects are resolved with lines converging at a single point on the horizon. This technique not only contributed to the field of architecture, but it affected the way people perceived art... Forever after.

An array of logistical issues cropped up throughout the construction of the dome. For example, the problem of how to get each piece of stone to the top of the building during construction arose. Brunelleschi

the yet non-existant Dome

the Campanile (Giotto's Bell Tower)

Basilica de Santa Maria del Fiore

Baptistry

◀ DOMELESS SHAME: *The pieces of the Cathedral Complex were built at different points in history. The Baptistery was built in 1059, the church was built in 1298, and the bell tower was built in 1359. The dome wasn't finished until 1436! The uncapped church created an air of shame and failure looming over the city - for 125 years! Until of course, Brunelleschi provided the necessary genius that allowed the eventual completion of il Duomo.*

GIANTS ~ THE PEOPLE

The Job Interview

How did Brunelleschi, who had never built anything of significance, actually get the all-important job of building the dome - ahead of his more experienced competitors?

Each person who entered the contest to build il Duomo, was asked how he would solve the overwhelming problems facing the construction of its dome. Most couldn't provide a satisfactory answer. When Brunelleschi was asked, he simply stated that it would be too complicated for him to explain. So he asked his inquirers to try to balance an egg on its end. But of course, they could not. So Brunelleschi took his egg, broke it gently on the table and the egg sat upright on its flat broken bottom.

"You cheated," they cried. To this, Brunelleschi stated that most difficult questions have answers that are obvious to those that understand, but may elude everyone else.

He was hired.

It's Party Time!

Upon the successful completion of il Duomo, it was time to celebrate. The city built a mile-long platform that began at the monastery of Santa Maria Novella, wound through the Florentine streets, and ended at the front door of the Church of Santa Maria del Fiore, the 'Duomo' church. Scaffolding was created to raise the entire length of the platform several feet off of the ground. It was decorated with colorful flowers and banners, and covered with a red fabric canopy.

At party time, the canopy-shaded Pope led the procession of cardinals, bishops and city officials along the extensive ramp to begin the triumphant celebration of the successful creation of the biggest dome in the entire world.

merely attached a pulley system to a few cattle so that when the cows walked in a circle, the *(cont.)* cradled stones would rise to the top. But bringing the cradle back down to the bottom for a refill proved difficult because it is challenging to get cattle to walk backwards.

To solve this problem, Brunelleschi invented the double-pulley system, so that when the cradle was unloaded at the top, they would simply switch the pulley to reverse the direction of the cradle, sending it back down to the bottom. The animals continued to walk in a single direction while the cradle travelled up and down as needed thereby solving that particular problem, and on he went.

These construction "issues" continued to crop up throughout the entire project until its glorious completion in 1436. The tempestuous Brunelleschi has been cherished ever since as the man that single-handedly changed the field of architecture for all time, and as the hero who kept the rain out of God's house.

Finding Brunelleschi Today

🌸 **il Duomo** is the flagship landmark touting the genius of Brunelleschi.

🌸 Across the piazza from the Duomo, you'll see Brunelleschi proudly gazing up at the product of his genius.

🌸 The Ospidale degli Innocenti (Hospital of the Innocent or Founding Hospital) was designed by Brunelleschi.

🌸 If you are politically inclined, you may enjoy seeing the Brunelleschi-designed Meeting Hall of the Guelph Party.

🌸 Brunelleschi designed the Old Sacristy in the Basilica San Lorenzo

🌸 The magnificent Basilica di Santo Spirito was re-designed by Brunelleschi to face the Arno. But city officials could not convince some citizens to relocate their homes, so the architects made it to face the opposite direction.

🌸 Brunelleschi designed the transport ship "il Badalone" (the Sea Monster) to carry heavy stone slabs up and down the Arno. Unfortunately, the ship sank on its first run. This model was found in the Baptistery office in Florence.

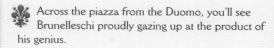

THE PEOPLE ~ GIANTS

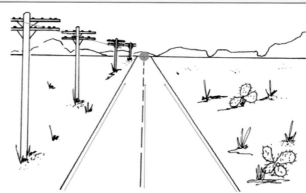

Linear: A Great Perspective

The concept of linear perspective, or vanishing point perspective as is it also known, has helped to solve the design of many types of projects, from complicated buildings and structures, to planning anything that required an 'eye' to see depth or distance. Today, this concept has advanced into what we know as 3D modeling, and is used in everything from design engineering to movie production. Thank you, Brunelleschi!

GHIBERTI
1378 - 1455

- Won a contest to build the doors of the Baptistery
- His doors were named "The Gates to Paradise"
- One of five 'Giants' whose work signaled massive change

Born 12 miles from Florence in the town of Pelago in 1378, Lorenzo di Cione Ghiberti (aka Lorenzo di Bartoluccio) was a designer, a sculptor, painter, goldsmith, architect and author.

Although his mother married Cione di Ghiberti, she left him and moved in with Bartoluccio di Michele who raised Lorenzo as his son. His step-father, a goldsmith himself, taught Lorenzo the intricacies of his craft. Lorenzo loved it so much that he quickly surpassed his step-father's skill level. In addition, Ghiberti made himself familiar with the art of casting with bronze, and in this too, he excelled. His curious nature led him to experiment with a variety of materials such as stucco and wax, and he excelled at the art of designing stained glass windows as well. His friends came to know that he was quite good at sketching, so they would often ask him to draw their likenesses as well.

In 1400, the plague once again reared its sickening head that encouraged Lorenzo to leave Florence. Gone only one year, Bartoluccio called him back to Florence because he heard that one of the merchant guilds was holding a contest to design and cast the new doors for the Baptistery di San Giovanni. They were looking for an artist to create a set of doors that would be similar to the existing south-side doors that were created by Andrea Pisano seventy years before. Bartoluccio felt this was a significant opportunity for Lorenzo to return to Florence and make a name for himself. And if he could win the competition, he would never have to create another pear-shaped pair of earrings again. So back to Florence he went, happily.

From the lot of applicants, the guild chose six masters to participate in the final competition. Besides Lorenzo, there were two other Florentines and three Tuscans. They were each given one year to create a panel that would illustrate their personal vision of the "Sacrifice of Isaac" in bronze. Lorenzo won the competition outright and set out to create the new doors to the Baptistery, which took him over 20 years to complete. It was said

THE PEOPLE ~ GIANTS

Architect ◆ Author ◆ Designer
Goldsmith ◆ Painter ◆ Sculptor

by Giorgio Vasari that "...the work was finished with such care that it seemed not cast and polished with iron tools but rather created by a breath."

During this 20-year period, he accepted a variety of other commissions along the way. These included the design and casting of three statues for three separate guilds to be housed in separate niches around the outside of the **Church of Orsanmichele**. He created "John the Baptist" for the Calimala, the same guild that chose him to create the doors. This sculpture is still considered to be one of his greatest works. He also cast "St. Matthew" for the Bankers' Guild and "St. Stephen" for the Wool Manufacturers' Guild.

He produced an unknown number of frescoes and stained glass windows as well as other bronze sculptures for a variety of patrons around the city. Meanwhile back at his workshop, he continued work on the Baptistery Doors providing the perfect learning environment for his students. Among others, they included the soon-to-be-famous **Donatello** and the already famous **Paolo Uccello**.

These north-side doors were created in the traditional Gothic form, each scene captured within a popular architectural shape known as a 'quatrefoil.'

"...Ghiberti in his work on the doors of San Giovanni... displays invention, order, style, and design, so that it seems as if his figures move and breathe." ~ Giorgio Vasari in "The Lives of the Artists"

Upon the completion of the doors, Ghiberti received such fame and notoriety that the guild had no difficulty selecting him once again to create the third set of doors for the East entrance of Baptistery di San Giovanni.

This time the job took him approximately 27 years, finishing in 1452, but the result was like nothing ever created since the time of the ancient Roman and Greek civilizations one thousand years earlier. Departing from the quatrefoil-encased scenes

North
2nd Doors were designed by Ghiberti 1401 - 1424

East
3rd Doors designed by Ghiberti "Gates to Paradise" 1425 - 1452

South
1st Doors were created by Pisano ~ 1330
Life of John the Baptist

Today you can walk around the Baptistery to enjoy the ingenious works of Pisano and later by Ghiberti.

GIANTS ~ THE PEOPLE

of the Gothic style, Ghiberti decided to go in an entirely different direction. These new scenes were each in squares that opened the space, giving him the freedom to create full stories within them. Ghiberti also chose the technique of creating depth of space using the method of linear perspective that had recently been invented by Brunelleschi. The doors were created with such innovative ingenuity and poignancy that Ghiberti's status was immediately elevated to a Master Artist.

Artists from all over the land came to see for themselves these creations that were so beautiful that Michelangelo was known to have said that they were not just ordinary doors, but they were truly the Gates to Paradise.

Ghiberti, who died a few short years after the completion of the doors, was entombed with the utmost honor and respect in the Church of Santa Croce in Florence. 🌼

THE ART OF COMPETITION
(or the Competition of the Art?)

When it came time to have a large, expensive and public piece of art commissioned, contests were held as the general method used to narrow down the difficult decision to create such pieces. After all, so much was at stake including local politics, religious politics, and public opinion not to mention the massive amounts of money required to complete these pieces. Oftentimes one of the local merchant's guilds was responsible for supervising this complex decision-making process.

In the case of 'ordering' the doors for the Baptistery was concerned, it was the "Arte de Calimala" (the Wool Cloth Merchants Guild) that held the honor of deciding who would receive the commission to build the doors, and what the reigning theme should be. Since the other entrance to the Baptistery already had doors created with a certain 'look and feel,' such as the depiction of biblical stories in barbed quatrefoil, it was agreed that the new doors should be of a similar ilk.

 **1.**  **2.**  **3.**

🌸 The Quatrefoil

This general shape was most commonly used as an architectural frame during the Gothic and early Renaissance years. There were three basic forms of quatrefoil: 1. basic quatrefoil shape. 2. basic quatrefoil with overlap, and 3. barbed quatrefoil. Architects were clever with the ways in which they incorporated the quatrefoil into their designs. Sometimes they would fill them with beautiful stained-glass designs and sometimes they would fill them with a story, as did both Brunelleschi and Ghiberti for their door panels shown opposite.

In 1401 the Calimala proposed a contest for the design and creation of the doors. Six men competed: Filippo di ser Brunellesci, Simone da Colle, Niccolò d'Arezzo, Jacopo della Quercia da Siena, Francesco di Valdombrina, and Nicholò Lamberti. The Guild narrowed this list down to two: Ghiberti and Brunelleschi. Their sample entries were to depict The Sacrifice of Isaac and they were each given one year to complete their competing samples.

Ghiberti's sample (left) succeeded over Brunelleschi's sample (right), and Ghiberti was given the commission to create the doors. However according to Manetti's account in his biography of Brunelleschi, the judges could not decide so they hired both of them to work together. But the temperamental Brunelleschi insisted that he would not take the commission unless it would be his and his alone, so they hired the more affable Ghiberti instead. Manetti also stated that Brunelleschi realized that, "because of his later victory in the completion of the Duomo, God had chosen wisely."

"Sacrifice of Isaac" by Ghiberti   "Sacrifice of Isaac" by Brunelleschi

Ghiberti had assistants to help him strong-arm the heavy tasks and to avoid the tedium. These assistants included his son Vittorio Ghiberti, and his later-famous students Paolo Uccello and Donatello. It took Ghiberti over 20 years to complete these doors, the result being a level of fame and fortune that he could never have previously imagined.

Soon after these doors were installed, another competition for the third set of doors had begun. But because of the overwhelming success of the second set, Ghiberti was unanimously chosen to receive the commission for the third. This new set of doors took him another 24 years to complete, and it is this set that, upon seeing them for the first time, Michelangelo called them "The Gates to Paradise."

The third set of doors has become one of the masterpieces that define the Renaissance, and has been used to teach and influence artists and architects alike thereafter.

POGGIO BRACCIOLINI
1380 - 1459

- Secretary to Pope John XXIII ('Pirate' Pope)
- Discovered a Pivotal Document by Lucretius
- Chancellor of Florence
- Known for his penmanship
- Created a lettering style that led to our cursive

Born Gian Francesco Poggio Bracciolini in the tiny Tuscan township of Terranuova (near Arezzo), Poggio grew up to become a mighty (albeit under-appreciated today) pillar that supported the solid foundation of the Renaissance Period, and buttressed the infrastructure of our modern thinking.

As a youth, young Poggio (pron PO-jo) studied Latin and law, while showing his innate love for writing. Not just books or stories in the beginning, but simply for handwriting. Penmanship. He became known for his beautiful connected flowing penmanship, an elegant but simple style that was

Engraving of Poggio Bracciolini by an unknown artist.

much easier to read than the typical broken script of the day. He took to copying manuscripts, letters, and contracts with rare speed and accuracy. In a time when few people were able to read - let alone write - Poggio was a rare find indeed, and his skills were in demand from an early age. These skills quickly earned him a position in the Notary's Guild. There, Poggio was paid handsomely to recreate documents for the city of Florence, for the Church, and for anyone else who had something to be copied, including his friend Cosimo (the Elder) de'Medici.

In Rome, Poggio worked side-by-side for 11 years with several Popes, most notably, Pope John XXIII - our "Pirate Pope." Later, after the abdication of Pope Gregory XII, Poggio was out of a job for 2 years. This left him free to pursue his life's passion of hunting ancient books.

Then when he was 56, Poggio met and married a 17-year-old girl, Selvaggia dei Buondelmonti. Despite receiving plenty of critism for marrying such a young girl, they bore 6 children together.

At 73, around the Fall of the Ottoman Empire, Poggio accepted the elite position as Chancellor of Florence, at the behest of his personal friend, Cosimo de' Medici.

Poggio was buried in the Basilica of Santa Croce in Florence, where today you will find a sculpture of him created by Donatello.

Highly recommended reading about Poggio: "The Swerve" by Stephen Greenblatt

Writer ◆ Humanist ◆ Politician
Historian ◆ Poet ◆ Scribe ◆ Book Hunter

THE GUSHER

During a 2-year respite from his papal secretarial duties, Poggio, around 1417, left Florence aboard his mule and rode north through the hills of what we know today as Switzerland, France, Austria and Germany. He was hunting for more of the rare books that, at the onset of the Fall of the Empire, the ancient Romans and Greeks hid in little monasteries which were scattered all throughout the remote Western European hills.

One day he came across a monastery with a little book room. He scoured their piles of books and came upon a simple nondescript writing entitled "De Rerum Natura," On The Nature Of Things. It was written by Lucretius, a then-unknown Roman philosopher. When Poggio opened the book, he knew instantly that he had found a treasure! He immediately took to hand-writing a copy of this book, and quickly proceeded back to Florence to share it with a few of his elite, educated friends.

This started a groundswell of rumblings as people secretly began to read about and understand such foreign, ancient, *and dangerous* topics as Epicureanism, atoms, and evolution. These secular ideas flew in the face of the knowledge that had been taught over the past 1,000 years of Dark Ages.

Over the next decades, people of wealth would have a copy of this book (and others) made for themselves, creating a means by which these concepts could spread. Quiet parlor-room discussions began popping up, all over Florence, and Rome, and ultimately Western Europe. But it was still dangerous to speak publicly about these dicey concepts. One could be severely punished for spreading such non-religious blather.

When a young Michelangelo listened quietly to these discussions from the corner of the Medici parlor, his head swirled with new images and concepts that demanded release through the only way he knew: his art. *(See Michelangelo "Making of a Maestro" on page 118)* This occurred repeatedly as other gifted artists began to express this new thinking through their own art. Great thinkers such as Machiavelli, Thomas More, Thomas Jefferson, and countless others were intensely inspired by these concepts.

This explosion of art and literature became the uproarious new voice of the people. *Giorgio Vasari* eventually came to call this uproar the "Renaissance."

Thus earning our friend Poggio (via Lucretius) the position as the pivotal person to awaken the world from what Petrarch called the "Dark Ages,' and create the gusher that ultimately led to the free-thinking Western cultures that we know today.

DONATELLO
1386 - 1466

- Created the first free-standing work in bronze
- Created the first nude statue since antiquity
- The only sculptor who could compete with Michelangelo
- One of five 'Giants' whose work signaled massive change

The son of a member of the Wool-combers Guild, Donatello di Niccolò di Betto Bardi was trained in the respectable art of Goldsmithing. During his younger years he hung out with a shy but funny self-taught engineer by the name of Filippo Brunelleschi. Both curious about the tales of fantastic buildings and statues created by the ancient Romans and Greeks from 1,000 years before, they spent several years in Rome passing every waking hour gazing at and studying the ancient buildings such as the Pantheon, the original St. Peter's Basilica and the Colosseum. Wanting to know every single crack and crevice of these buildings, they were seen laying on the ground drawing images in the dirt and discussing for all hours of the night. Donatello studied them from an artistic perspective, and Brunelleschi, from an architectural point of view. Properly inspired by the ancients, they returned to Florence. Brunelleschi was ready to take on the architectural problems of the Duomo that had plagued the city for over 125 years, and of course Donatello went on to become known as the only sculptor "that could compete with Michelangelo."

DONATELLO

Perfection and Concession

One day, after Donatello had created a wooden Crucifix. He asked his trusted friend Brunelleschi to give him an opinion of it. Brunelleschi said, "It looks as though it is a pauper upon the cross; it does not have the beauty & perfection that Christ should have." Donatello, angered, said, "Well if you can do better, here is a piece of wood. Make one yourself."

Three months later, Donatello and Brunelleschi were walking home from the market together. Brunelleschi said, "Here is the key to my house. Go there and wait for me. I will be along shortly." Upon entering, Donatello saw a crucifix sitting in the middle of the room - and it was PERFECTION! He was so aghast that his hands relaxed and released the part of his frock that was holding fresh eggs and vegetables for their lunch. Brunelleschi entered and said, "What is your plan, Donatello? How can we have a meal if you have dropped all of our food on to the floor?" Donatello, looking at the beautiful crucifix, replied, "I am clearly intended to carve only a pauper, while you are intended to carve perfection."

Goldsmith ✦ Stone Sculptor ✦ Bronze Sculptor

Stmark Licensed under Creative Commons Attribution Share Alike 3.0 via Wikimedia Commons
http://commons.wikimedia.org/wiki/File:Stmark.jpg#mediaviewer/File:Stmark.j

The Clever Chisel

For the Linen-draper's Guild, Donatello was asked to create a sculpture of St. Mark (along with Brunelleschi) which never quite transpired. He spent months chiseling, hammering and scraping. When the sculpture was unveiled, the members of the guild did not react well. They were not comfortable with some of the proportions: the elongated arms, the over-sized hands, etc. He argued that it was created to be viewed from below, and that it would appear more pleasing once it was erected and placed high - which is where it was intended to be seen. But still they were not happy. He told them that he would make careful changes and adjustments; so he covered it again for 15 more days. More chiseling and hammering could be heard. This time once uncovered, they were quite ecstatic with the new results and were happy to raise it and place it up where it was meant to be. And all was well.

P.S. When he had covered it up for those last 15 days, Donatello actually made no changes to it at all. He merely made them believe that he was making careful changes and adjustments. Then he actually unveiled the exact same version that everyone saw the first time.   ;-)

GIANTS ~ THE PEOPLE

The Bean Merchant

Cosimo (the Elder) de' Medici had a great fondness and admiration for Donatello's genius. And in turn, Donatello held Cosimo in high esteem and considered him a good friend. Because of Cosimo's wealthy connections, he was able to find new work for Donatello, and he was able to pay him during the creation of these works until the buyer paid for the piece upon the completion of a project.

One day, a bean merchant from Genoa asked Donatello to create a life-sized bronze head in such a way as to make it light enough to be transported a long distance to its destination without damage. Upon completion, Donatello told the merchant the price. The man scoffed stating that the price was much too high. "Nonsense," interjected Cosimo. "In fact, Donatello's price is way too low!" The merchant stated that it took only a single month to create it and that he should only have to pay a single month's wage. An insulted Donatello immediately turned and shoved the statue out the window watching as it shattered in the street below. To the merchant he said, "Sir, you are clearly much better at bargaining for beans than for art!" Aghast, the merchant begged Donatello to recreate the head for twice the price, but Donatello stoutly refused.

David, Goliath & Florence

The topic of "David and Goliath" was ever-popular during the Renaissance period. Many interpretations of "David" have been created with a variety of media by a host of artists and sculptors. "David" is the allegorical representation of Florence as the power of good over evil, right versus might, the little guy against a big bully.

Donatello's David was quite famous for nearly a century before Michelangelo created his own version of David.

Finding Donatello Today

🌸 **Piazza della Signoria** The story of "Judith and Holofernes" comes from the Bible's Book of Judith. In Donatello's illustration in bronze (below), Judith creeps into an Assyrian camp, captivates Holofernes with her beauty, gets him very drunk, and cuts off his head.

🌸 **Museo dell'Opera del Duomo** Donatello's ultra-realistic wooden sculpture of Mary Magdalene (right) was immediately well-received in Florence. The detailed way in which her starvation and penitence is poignantly created had never been seen with this amount of sensitivity.

🌸 **The Bargello** You will find Donatello's most famous version of "David" (left) in bronze.

🌸 **The Bargello** Donatello's earlier creation of "David" in marble also resides at the Bargello.

🌸 Outside the **Uffizi Gallery** you will find a sculpture of Donatello himself among the line-up of famous Renaissance Giants.

🌸 **Orsanmichele,** exterior, near the center of the historical district of Florence, you will find a copy of Donatello's sculpture of St. Mark in one of the niches. The interior collection includes the original.

🌸 **Museo dell'Opera del Duomo** Donatello's Statue of St. John the Evangelist.

🌸 **Basilica Santa Croce** Donatello's sculpture of "The Annunciation."

THE PEOPLE ~ GIANTS

81

FRA ANGELICO
1395 - 1455

GIANTS ~ THE PEOPLE

- The most prolific fresco artist from the Renaissance period
- Gifted the Pope with illuminations
- Favored artist of Cosimo (the elder) de' Medici

Baptized in 1395 as Guido (or Guidolino) di Pietro, he possessed a kind and quiet disposition. Although his talent attracted attention to him at an early age, he nevertheless felt that he would like to enter the monastery to serve God in a way that he believed would garner less attention. So to accommodate his own peace of mind, he entered The Order of the Preaching Friars and became Fra Giovanni of Fiesole - Angelic Brother John of the town of **Fiesole**.

Not much is known about Guido's early days, but it is known that when he entered the Monastery, he was already an artist. Like his brother, he had been trained as a manuscript 'illuminator' and eventually his talents evolved toward frescoes.

Fra Angelico was admired by Cosimo (the 'Elder') de' Medici. After asking Michelozzo to rebuild the Church of San Marco, he invited Fra Giovanni (Angelico) to decorate it. Word spread of his talents, which

Fra Angelico in the painting "Deeds of the Antichrist" by Luca Signorelli

were appreciatively coupled with his modest and gentle disposition so that he was gainfully employed all over the cities of Florence and Fiesole.

He worked in nearly every place of worship in town including the Churches of San Marco, Santa Trinità, San Francesco (outside the San Miniato Gate), Santa Maria Novella and of course in his own residence of San Domenico in Fiesole, as well as nearly every parish and place of worship in the visible distance. He also decorated inside so many homes of the citizens of Florence that Vasari, in his book ***"Lives of the Artists"*** wondered "...how one man could have possibly executed so much work that is perfect."

Word of his talents and easy disposition spread down to Rome so that one day Pope Nicholas requested his presence. The Pope wished for Angelico to decorate within the Vatican, which he did in good order. He decorated the chapel where the Pope hears Mass

Virgin and Child with Saints, Fiesole (1428–1430)

Friar ◆ Painter ◆ Illuminator

What is an "Illuminator"?

During the middle ages and later into the Renaissance, a manuscript or document that had been decorated with silver or gold was referred to as an illumination. Today the term refers to any decorated or illustrated manuscript.

with a Deposition of the Cross as well as a variety of scenes from the life of St. Lawrence. While there, he also gifted the Pope with a number of the Pope's own books which Fra Angelico beautifully illuminated. Vasari added that "all the saints in his paintings are so lifelike and have such sweet and delicate expressions that the entire coloring of this work seems to have come from the hand of such a saint or angel as these. Thus, this good Friar was always called Brother Giovanni 'Angelico' (the Angelic Brother John) with very good reason." And hence his nickname of 'Fra Angelico' has replaced all of his other names for 600 years. 🌼

◀ *"The Annunciation"*
The wall in the background represents the walls within the chamber where this image was created.by Fra Angelico and creates a beautiful 'trompe l'oeil'.

MICHELOZZO
1396 - 1472

- Fled Florence in loyalty to Cosimo de' Medici
- Redesigned the Great Monastery of San Marco
- Built the walls around Dubrovnik, Croatia
- Designed & built the Medici Palace
- Often teamed with Donatello

Michelozzo de Bartolomeo Michelozzi was born in
Florence to a tailor, and was one of the more fortunate
up-and-coming young artists. His raw talents made
him an obvious choice to study under the great master
artist Ghiberti. From 1425-1434, Michelozzo formed a
partnership with Donatello and together they completed an
extensive assortment of projects that included the sculpture
of St. Matthew outside of Orsanmichele.

Along the way, a young Michelozzo was befriended by
none other than Cosimo (the Elder) de' Medici, who found
the personal creativity of Michelozzo to be of a rare quality.
They became lifelong friends and Michelozzo's loyalty to
Cosimo went so
far as to bring him
to accompany him
to Venice during
the Medici exile
from Florence.

This image, taken from Fra
Angelico's "Deposition
of Christ," is said to be that of
Michelozzo.

> When Michelozzo built the
> Wall around Dubrovnik, Croatia,
> it was heralded as one of the
> greatest fortification systems
> of the Middle Ages, as it was
> never breached by hostile forces
> during this time period.

Michelozzo felt that if the city did not want Cosimo,
then they probably would not miss his best friend
either. During their stay in Venice, Michelozzo
designed the Library of San Giorgio Maggiore to please
his Medici friend.

One year later, when Cosimo was triumphantly
asked to return to Florence, Michelozzo too was
ecstatic to return to his own home town, basking in
the success of his benefactor.

Because Michelozzo was his favored architect,
Cosimo paid him handsomely to design the Medici
Palace (known today as the "Palazzo Medici
Ricardi"). His insightful design of the Palace became
the defacto standard in Palace design for the next
one hundred years.

Michelozzo died at the age of 72 and is interred
appropriately in the monastery of his beautiful
Church of San Marco in Florence. 🌼

Goldsmith ◆ Clay Sculptor ◆ Bronze Sculptor
Stone Sculptor ◆ Inventor ◆ Businessman

which he was comfortable working. This approach worked financially because he was able to accept more work and finish in a far shorter amount of time.

But there were still a few problems. Mainly that clay did not stand up well to time or weather. And he wanted his work to appear more lifelike. So he developed paints that worked well with clay and began producing intricate and colorful works - using only two to three colors on any given piece.

Continuing to assuage his experimental nature, he developed a fine clear glaze that was easy to fire and held up beautifully in the harsh weather all the while protecting the integrity of his pieces.

This is just one part of the 10-piece "Cantoria," one of Luca's earliest commissioned pieces in marble. It was created before he evolved into his later works in glazed terracotta clay.

His workshop began operating at full speed. Luca encouraged his brother to quit his day job and persuaded him to come to work in his shop. Together they doubled production and significantly more than doubled their earnings.

Luca's unique technique of glazed clay had caught on extensively, and orders were rolling in from all over Europe. In order to accommodate them, he created molds and templates that would enable him to produce pieces in a higher volume and in a shorter amount of time. He then devised a clever way for them to be assembled upon delivery to the client, which in turn, led him

to inventing better and smaller packaging in order to ship his products less expensively and more efficiently.

Passing his skills to a variety of family members, he knew that the della Robbia workshop would survive long after his own death. His nephew Andrea became quite well-known with his own terracotta works as did Andrea's own son Giovanni.

Luca della Robbia is remembered not only for creating emotionally poignant works of art, but because he developed and mastered a new medium during a time when the rest of the art world was busy reviving techniques and styles from the ancients. ❧

All throughout the Basilica of Santa Croce, you will find the unique and colorful terracotta creations from the family della Robbia.

GIANTS ~ THE PEOPLE

MASACCIO
1401 - 1427/28

- Mastered the use of perspective
- First to paint a nude body in over 1,000 years
- Greatly influenced Michelangelo, da Vinci, etc.
- One of five 'Giants' whose work signaled massive change

For a man that lived a mere 27 years, Masaccio's contribution to the Renaissance movement was colossal. Born as Tommaso di ser Giovanni di Simone Cassai in Florence, he became known by his peers as the fifth of the five Giants whose excellent works signalled to the world that a change was surely afoot.

Born in Arezzo in 1401, Masaccio daringly parted ways with the traditional 'flat' Gothic form of art. Once he learned the value of using "vanishing point" techniques from his friend Brunelleschi, he pushed forth to perfect this technique without ever looking back. His work had a monumental impact on other artists henceforth. For his audacity, he has earned his rightful position as one of the five great artists that gave birth to the Renaissance.

Masaccio's self-portrait from his "Raising of the Son of Theophilus and St Peter Enthroned" can be found in the Brancacci Chapel. p216

In addition, he was one of the very first artists to paint the human body in its nude form in over 1,000 years. Unlike Michelangelo and da Vinci, Masaccio did not learn about the internal intricacies of the human body that make us look the way we do on the outside. This lack of internal knowledge left his paintings looking a bit too smooth and not quite realistic. However, it is still clear, that through his art, he ventured into a no-man's land of the discovery of the human body.

When his favorite patron and dear friend Cosimo (the Elder) de' Medici was exiled, Masaccio, no longer feeling at home in Florence, moved to Rome to further his artistic education and experience. While there he received commissions from important art lovers such as the work he did in the Vatican for Pope Martin. Later, upon hearing that Cosimo had been invited to return back to Florence from his exile, Masaccio himself returned to his beloved Florence.

"Masaccio was very absent-minded and unpredictable, like a man who has devoted his whole life and will only to the details of art, caring very little about himself and even less about others." His nickname of 'Masaccio' can be translated as 'Messy Thomas' or 'Clumsy Thomas.'
Giorgio Vasari in *Lives of the Artists*

Some of his better-known frescoes are still exhibited today in Florence's Brancacci Chapel inside the Church of Santa Maria del Carmine. Throughout the Renaissance, artists flocked to the Brancacci Chapel in order to study the superb techniques evident in Masaccio's art. It is known that of those artists, the few that eventually worked in this Chapel themselves, grew to heights of unparalleled fame. These included such greats as Raphael, Fra Angelico, Fra

Goldsmith ◆ Bronze Sculptor
Stone Sculptor ◆ Inventor ◆ Entrepreneur

Lippi and his son Filippino Lippi, Andrea del Verrocchio, Ghirlandaio, Sandro Botticelli and even Leonardo da Vinci. It is said that although Michelangelo has taught thousands of artists through his works, he himself was taught by Masaccio.

Dying abruptly of unknown causes at the dismally young age of 27, many have wondered if these causes may have included poison. But murder has never since been proven. His death came as a shock to the artistic community who made sure that his work was properly preserved and that his genius would never be forgotten. 🌸

The Trinity

This painting was discovered in the Church of Santa Maria Novella in 1860, hiding behind an altar designed by Giorgio Vasari in 1568. Knowing and respectful of the genius of Masaccio, Vasari, an artist in his own right, designed the altar to be built in front of this painting leaving a gap between them to provide a protection for the painting.

One of the more interesting points of this piece is that upon entering this space in the church and seeing this painting on the wall, for a moment your eye is tricked (trompe l'oeil) into thinking that it is a real extension of the room in which you are standing. By creating that very complex domed ceiling, he is almost boasting his mastery in the use of linear perspective that lends to the super-realism of this piece.

The Trinity is represented by God the Father, the Son Jesus, and the Holy Ghost that is depicted by the White Dove (looks like God is wearing a white collar). Below this scene is an open casket or tomb with a skeleton upon it. Above the skeleton is an inscription in Latin that translates to "I am as you will be, and you are as I once was." This is taken to mean that death is inevitable to us all.

Finding Masaccio Today	🌸 Inside the Basilica Santa Maria del Carmine - *the Brancacci Chapel*	🌸 Galleria degli Uffizi
	🌸 Santa Maria Novella	🌸 San Pietro, Cascia di Reggello (Florence)

THE PEOPLE ~ GIANTS

FILIPPO LIPPI
1406 - 1469

- Kidnapped by Barbary pirates; held in slavery
- Prolific and inventive with his frescoes
- Instructor to Sandro Botticelli

Filippo Lippi was raised by his aunt (his father's sister) because his parents died when he was very young. His aunt fell into difficult times and could not afford to raise him alone. So when young Filippo was eight years old, she had him enter the monastery of the Carmelite Friars in the Carmine Church. He was not a good student and did not find that reading and writing were in his nature. Instead, he would sketch crudely on his books as well as those of this classmates. His teacher decided that if drawing is what Filippo wanted to do, then drawing he would do. He gave the boy plenty of opportunities to draw, sketch and paint. In Masaccio's chapel, each day he joined with other boys who also enjoyed drawing, and it was soon found that his skills surpassed all of theirs. It seemed to be common knowledge among those that knew him that he would grow up to be a famous artist. At the age of 16, he took his vows and became a friar.

Self portrait of Fra Filippo Lippi in his "Coronation of the Virgin."

In the chapel, he utilized a style called "terra verde" (green earth - a method used in monochromatic art) to create a painting of a Pope confirming the rule of the Carmelites. In addition he painted a variety of frescoes that garnered him a massive amount of attention and praise. In fact, he had so beautifully attained Masaccio's touch and was able to mirror his works so closely that some folks said that Masaccio's spirit had moved into Lippi's body.

KIDNAPPED!

One day while young Filippo and his buddies were passing the afternoon in a little boat, they were attacked by a Moorish ship and taken to Barbary where they were chained and forced to live in discomfort and slavery. Eighteen months had passed in this condition, when Filippo one day sketched a portrait of his new master. The man was awestruck because he had never seen his own likeness! In this place, art, by and large, was unavailable. Feeling that this boy was truly a gift from the heavens and not something to be owned, he set young Filippo free.

When he was 17 years old, he had amassed enough praise for his work that he decided that he did not want to be a monk anymore, and left the monastery. However, it is believed that he was never actually released from his vows.

Throughout his life, he was quite famous and of course, well paid. However, in a letter dated in 1439, he described himself as the "...poorest friar in Florence..." Some feel this perpetual state of poverty was self-inflicted due to his willingness to part with his money every time a woman entered his life, those of which were many.

Filippo earned the attention of Cosimo (the Elder) de' Medici with whom he formed a lifelong friendship. This friendship included the continued patronage of his art by the Medici and a

Goldsmith ✦ Bronze Sculptor ✦ Painter
Stone Sculptor ✦ Inventor ✦ Entrepreneur

A Show of Hands

Early in his illustrious career as a painter, Fra Lippi found his work still being criticized because the hands of some of the people in his works didn't look quite real. He apparently wasn't able to fix this problem, so he decided to do the next best thing: whenever the figures in his paintings had hands showing, he would neatly and cleverly cover them up with a draped cloth, or some other device that would otherwise look quite natural in each particular scene. Some say that this is but one way to determine which part of his life a painting was created.

Lucrezia Buti

One day Lippi was asked to paint a Madonna and Child. He spotted a beautiful young woman and asked the nuns if she could be his model for the painting. With their approval, he took the young Lucrezia Buti to his house where he had relations with her and would not let her return to the convent, no matter how vehemently the nuns requested, then protested. Filippo was in love. Lucrezia was the model for many of his paintings and eventually bore him a son whom they named Filippo. Little Filippino grew up to be as famous an artist as his father.

constant introduction to high-ranking individuals who were quite happy to pay dearly for Lippi's works. Considered to be one of the more prolific artists of the Renaissance, Lippi worked in most every church and chapel in Florence and surrounds, where today many of his pieces can still be enjoyed. He died in the city of Spoleto during the creation of a fresco in the Spoleto cathedral. ✿

The solid flat haloes (a left-over from the Byzasntine style) seen in this "Madonna and Child" indicate that this piece was created early in Lippi's career. Later, he innovated the art of 'translucence' into his paintings. (See "Madonna" next page.)

This piece was created much later in his career as indicated by the transparent halo and the realism in the shading of the skin in this "Madonna and Child." The real-life setting inspired other artists to also create biblical scenes within realistic settings.

THE PEOPLE ~ GIANTS

Lippi's "Coronation of the Virgin" which currently resides in the Uffizi, possesses several features worth noting: Instead of the traditional Byzantine method of illuminating the sky with gold, Lippi chose to repre-sent the sky as blue stripes. The 'stage' (lower-front-center) because it is raised, creates a perfect triangle that peaks at the head of the Virgin, a typical trait in Renaissance art. Lower-left: notice the man with his chin resting on his hand: this is Lippo Lippi himself.

Cosimo de' Medici once hired Lippo to do some work in his home, knowing that Lippo could become so obsessed by his personal passions that he would pay no attention to his work. So Cosimo locked him into a room and told him to paint. After two days, Lippo cut his bed sheets into strips and used them to climb out the window. After several days Cosimo's men successfully returned him to the Medici, where Cosimo decided that Lippo would be happier and more productive if not confined. Having the option of coming or going was now a privilege for Lippo, at which point he decided to stay until the conclusion of his work for his friend Cosimo.

*This "Madonna & Child with Two Angels" is considered to be one of Filippo's most endearing and enduring paintings. Lippo (Filippo's nickname) depicts the Child being supported by the angels rather than the Madon-na. Many believe that the model for this Madonna was Lucrezia Buti, Filippo's lover. Notice that the nearly invisible halo replaces the traditional thicker halo or the ethereal glow surrounding the Madonna's head. Her veil realistically lacks opacity which makes it appear almost invisible. It also includes the exquisite detail of every individual stitch around its edge. It is clear that the old Byzantine style of art is now gone as Lippi uses delicate shading to depict both depth and realism rather than the old flat style. The curls of the angel's hair give a sense of playfulness, as does the depth of color in the corona of his eyes. Notice that the Madonna and the angel possess an air of sweetness. This practice of creating 'happy' people was immediately adopted by other Renaissance artists. Sandro Botticelli, a favored student of Lippi, later used these techniques to display happiness and beauty in his own paintings. This extraordinary painting (tempera on wood) can be enjoyed today in the **Uffizi Gallery.***

THE PEOPLE ~ GIANTS

ANDREA DEL VERROCCHIO
1435 - 1488

- Grand Master whose students included Leonardo da Vinci
- Created the second of the three famous "Davids"

Born Andrea di Michele di Francesco de' Cioni, he was trained under a master goldsmith, Giuliano Verrocchio, from whom Andrea took the name, which translates to "true eyes." He grew up with Lorenzo de' Medici as a close friend. Although a bachelor for life, he lived with and supported his sister and her children.

For quite some time, Verrocchio was considered to be one of the most important artists in Florence. Lorenzo and Piero de' Medici were Verrocchio's chief patrons that paid handsomely for Verrocchio's works of art. The Medici supporters also contributed dearly toward a very successful school of art, run by Verrocchio himself. Critics have since argued which paintings Verrocchio actually created himself. This has caused some turmoil in the valuations of some of his individual works of art today.

Some of his students grew to altogether new heights of fame, glory and wealth. His stand-out students include Pietro Perugino (who trained Raphael), Lorenzo di Credi (who shaped da Vinci's early work, then later was influenced by da Vinci), da Vinci himself, Domenico Ghirlandaio (who also taught grand masters Leonardo da Vinci, Botticelli, and the Renaissance grand master himself, Michelangelo).

A sculptor, Andrea designed the funerary monument of Cosimo de' Medici and the crypts of Piero and Giovanni de' Medici. Today they can be seen in the Medici Chapel in Florence. In 1468, Verrocchio accepted the task of creating the golden sphere for the top of the Duomo. This process involved soldering together many sheets of copper, hammering them into place, then gilding them with gold. The ball was struck by lightening in 1601 and quickly repaired by 1602. [The cross on top of the ball was made by someone else.]

One day, while Verrocchio was painting his "Baptism of Christ" he asked one of his students to paint one of the angels, while Andrea painted the other one. Can you tell which was painted by his student? **Answer:** this student was a young Leonardo da Vinci, whose angel has a more ethereal beauty than Verrocchios more earthy-looking angel.

Verrocchio died while working on a statue of General Bartolomeo Colioni in Venice. And so he never saw its completion. The statue was eventually finished by Alessandro Leopardi and stands today in the Campo SS Giovanni e Paolo in Venice.

Painter ◆ Goldsmith ◆ Bronze Sculptor

I shall never paint again!

When Master Verrocchio saw the first complete painting from his young student Leonardo da Vinci, he was so taken aback by its perfect beauty and by the raw talent, skill and genius of this young Leonardo, that he vowed he would never pick up a brush again!

HOW TO MAKE A BRONZE STATUE

Using The Lost Wax Method

1. A stick-figure made from a metal wire (coat hanger?) is formed into the general shape of the statue.

2. Clay is then built up onto the wire, and hand-molded into the general shape and size of the statue.

3. Next, a thin layer of wax is applied, cooled until it hardens, then it is carved into the perfectly detailed finished product ~ hair, eyelashes, all details.

4. A heavy coat of plaster is then applied over the beautifully-carved wax layer. Remember: the inside of the plaster is taking the perfect shape of the wax layer inside it. Several holes are made in the plaster where the bronze will enter and the wax will exit.

5. Once the plaster is good and dry, hot molten liquid bronze is poured into holes in the top, melting the wax into liquid which will drain out through holes on the bottom.

6. When the bronze is completely cooled and hardened, the plaster mold will be broken away leaving a perfectly-formed bronze statue (we hope!).

7. Sharp edges of bronze that may remain from the molding process are filed off, and the statue is polished to the artist's desired smoothness.

For Verrocchio's beautiful "David" statue (located in The Bargello), he cast the head of Goliath separately from the main statue. Although the hilt of the sword that you see on this statue was part of the original casting, the sword blade itself was replaced much later during a restoration. Being trained as a goldsmith, Verrocchio painted molten gold in various places on the statue to give it the final luster.

❧

BOTTICELLI
1445 - 1510

- Considered to be one of the greatest artists of all time
- Painter of "Primavera" and the "Birth of Venus"
- Personal friend and confidante to the Medici family
- Lost some of his works in the Bonfire of the Vanities

Sandro (Alessandro di Mariano di Vanni Filipepi) Botticelli was born in Florence and was initially taught the respected art of goldsmithing by his older brother. During his teenage years, his talents as a painter became apparent and eventually his early works were noticed by some of the then-current masters. He was apprenticed by art Maestro Fra Filippo Lippi, and Lippi's 'sweet and happy' influence can be seen in many of Botticelli's works.

Sandro maintained an art studio (workshop) in Florence in which his customers would either purchase his 'on the shelf' items (one of the more popular items were his paintings of the Madonna & Child on wooden panels), or they would order custom paintings directly from Sandro himself.

Botticelli was well-known for the clarity of vision in his paintings. He loved to paint what he saw in real life and from nature, from Greek legends and from his own imagination. Often the people in his paintings held expressions of sweetness, happiness and joy, a direct line back to the influence of his teacher Filippo Lippi.

▲ *With his lackadaisical eyes and heart-shaped lips, this is an unmistakable self-portrait of Sandro Botticelli as he appears in his "Adoration of the Magi."*

Botticelli means "Little Barrel." This nickname was originally given to his 'stout' older brother, but for some unknown reason, it ended up with Sandro ~ who wasn't really very stout at all ~ but it stuck.

One day, a Dominican monk came to town spouting the ways of the Lord in a loud fiery-brimstone manner. This monk, Girolamo Savonarola, dogmatically cursed people to hell who did not live up to his personal vision of devout followers of the Lord. He had the rare ability to bully people by using guilt - his chief weapon of choice - into climbing aboard his band wagon. And lo, he gathered quite a following of both devout as well as fence-sitting Florentines. If you had no desire to spend eternity in the fiery pits of hell, then you must cast your worldly goods into a fire. These goods included stylish clothing, fancy furniture, artwork and silver as well as many other items considered by Savonarola the devil's distractions. He created huge bonfires in the Piazza della Signoria - right in the center of town. Citizens came out in droves to prove their devoutness by throwing their 'stuff' into the bonfire. The bigger or more valuable the items, the more devout you proved yourself to be. Botticelli always considered himself to be a loyal Christian, but Savonarola's harsh words and tones penetrated even Botticelli's God-given talents: It is said that Sandro threw some of his own paintings (quite valuable even then) into the fire and pursued an extra-pious living by painting more religious topics, as can be seen by a noticeable change in his style at about that time. Sadly, an unknown number of Botticelli's works were destroyed in these **"Bonfires of the Vanities."**

Like Michelangelo, Botticelli was intrigued by the tales of the ancient Greeks and Romans that were 'in vogue' during the Medici reign. This can be seen in many of his paintings, most notably in his 'take' on the annual rebirth of nature in the 'Primavera' and the "Birth of Venus."

GIANTS ~ THE PEOPLE

Master Painter ◆ Gold Smith

Sandro Botticelli's "Inferno Canto" and the
"Abyss of Hell" have become known as the

'official' visualizations of Dante's concept of Hell,
and are still seen this way today.

With the new century rolling firmly into place (the 1500's), and with his chums **Lorenzo & Giulliano** both deceased, Sandro fell under the spell of Savonarola. Artistic flavors were shifting to a more 'mannerist' style, Botticelli's work fell out of fashion and his business dried up. All of these circumstances changed his outlook on the world and affected his output as well. Even though his art was being considered as 'old school,' the upper social echelon of Florence still revered him as a Renaissance master. Botticelli died in peace at 65 years of age. 🌸

Bride-ophobia?
Botticelli was known to have stated that the prospect of marriage gave him nightmares. This was one of the things that contributed to accusations of sodomy. But because of a lack of evidence, and because this accusation was a common tactic used by competitors, all charges were dropped.

Was Lorenzo de' Medici's handsome younger brother Giuliano
used as the model for the only male in "Primavera"?

"Primavera" aka "The Allegory of Spring," represents goodness (humanism?), the ideal of a positive confidence that is sensitive to the needs of others. This reflects well Botticelli's feelings towards the Medici. It was created for a cousin of Lorenzo the Magnificent: Lorenzo di Pierfrancesco de' Medici.

The Adoration of Botticelli

GIANTS ~ THE PEOPLE

Although his reputation had deteriorated for nearly 300 years after his death, Botticelli's work has since been reanalyzed and determined to be some of the best representations of the linear grace of the Renaissance style. As such, his "Birth of Venus" and "La Primavera" have become some of the most reproduced pieces of art in history to date.

Young Lorenzo the Magnificent *(approx age 15)*   Cosimo *(the Elder)* de' Medici   Joseph, Mary & the infant Jesus   Piero & Giovanni de' Medici *(Cosimo's sons)*   the Owner of this Painting   Sandro Botticelli *(Self Portrait)*

"Adoration of the Magi" - Currently hangs in the Uffizi Gallery.

Botticelli enjoyed a lifelong close and personal relationship with the Medici family. This relationship was a key element in the durable popularity of his work. Many people who wished to garner favor from the Medici would stumble over themselves to purchase a Botticelli painting. One such notable example was a tax collector, who wished to endear himself to the Medici family by ordering a painting called the "Adoration of the Magi" (above) which has since become infamous for its political statements. Instead of a more traditional religious setting, Botticelli chose to set the scene amid an ancient Roman ruin made of stone. Sandro, aware that the Medici considered themselves to be the modern-day Magi, featured the Medici family prominently as they gathered around Christ. Botticelli placed a self-portrait in the painting. The remainder are people who were part of the Medici 'cognoscenti' or inner circle.

The "Birth of Venus" is the first example (in Tuscany) of a painting on canvas. Commissioned by the Medici, it beautifully represents the gentle grace of the traditional Renaissance style.

Throughout the coloring process, Botticelli strengthened the contours by means of a pointed instrument, probably to give them the bold clarity so characteristic of his recognizable Renaissance style.

Simonetta Vespucci was the model for "The Birth of Venus" as well as many other Botticelli works. Even after her death, Botticelli still included Vespucci in some of his paintings. At his behest, he was buried at her feet in the Church of Ognisanti in Florence when he died in 1510. Was Sandro in love with her? Perhaps...

Botticelli based his Venus (above) on an ancient Roman sculpture of a "Modest" Venus, which existed in his time in the Medici collection.

Finding Botticelli Today

 in Italia
The Uffizzi Gallery, Florence
Accademia, Florence
Pitti Palace, Florence
Ognissanti, Florence: St Augustine

Museo Poldi Pezzoli, Milan, Italy
Museo Nazionale, Arezzo, Italy
Biblioteca Ambrosiana, Milan, Italy

Vatican Museum, Roma
Sistine Chapel, Roma
Galleria Pallavicini, Roma
Accademia Carrara, Bergamo, Italy

Internationale
The Louvre, Paris
National Gallery, DC, USA
Metropolitan Museum of Art, NYC, USA
University of Harvard, Cambridge, USA
Pushkin Museum/Fine Art, Moscow, Rus
Staatliche Museen, Berlin, Germany
Prado Museum, Spain
São Paulo Museum of Art, São Paulo, Brz
National Gallery, London, England
British Museum, London, England
Städelsches Kunstinstitut, Frankfurt, Ger
Alte Pinakothek, Munich, Germany
Beaverbrook Mus, NB, Canada

THE PEOPLE ~ GIANTS

101

GHIRLANDAIO
1449 - 1494

- Instructor to da Vinci, Botticelli, Michelangelo, etc.
- First to focus on the background within a painting
- Perfected the use of directional lighting

Domenico di Tommaso di Currado di Doffo Bigordi was the eldest of six children, and one of the three who survived to adulthood. He apprenticed with his father who was a fairly well-known goldsmith. Although Domenico showed exceptional skills and talents with metals, he was often distracted with drawing. He drew everything. To pass the time, he would quickly draw the likenesses of individuals as they casually passed by the workshop. It astounded people that he could so quickly capture their image without having to sit and pose, as was required by the other more traditional artists.

As both his interest and his experience broadened, he became known first for his frescoes (paintings on wet plaster), then for the ease that he took in painting directly onto dry walls. He possessed a unique style that would place saints and biblical figures into everyday settings, and all within the proper arrangement so as to correctly represent the appropriate biblical story. The backgrounds of his paintings were just as important as the foregrounds. This unique style quickly caught on and became his vehicle to widespread fame. Gone were the days of idealistic art; by that time realism had clearly taken hold as the highest-paying genre that was most favored by patrons, and Ghirlandaio was certainly one of the most loved artists of his time. 🌸

> Domenico was the first to utilize "garlands" in the hair of girls and young women in his paintings. This caught on with other painters who also found creativity in the use of floral crowns. It was from this practice that Domenico acquired the nickname that stuck with him throughout eternity: "Ghirlandaio".

St. Jerome in his Study 1480
Church of Ognissanti, Florence

"Adoration of the Shepards" 1485. Contains Ghirlandaio's self-portrait.

"The Adoration of the Magi" 1488-89, Hospital of the Innocent, Florence

Goldsmith ◆ Characaturist
Master Renaissance Instructor

◀ The "Birth of Mary" (or "Nativity of the Madonna") is set in an ornately decorous room. On the bed is St. Anne while she watches the women bathe her new baby. She is visited by a small group of friends, one pregnant. The light coming through the chamber window, although common, demonstrates Ghirlandaio's technique of using directional lighting to give meaning to controlled shadowing which was not commonly found in earlier Renaissance paintings.

Ghirlandaio's fresco of "The Last Supper" (1480) is in the refectory of the Church of Ognissanti in Florence today. It is set around an ornate table on the evening that Jesus announces to his apostles that one of them will betray him. This perspective gives the illusion of looking up into the arched ceiling, a technique called 'sotto in su.' Ghirlandaio does not disappoint with the attention paid to the details of the setting: the quails flying over the orange trees, the intricate embroidery at the ends of the tablecloth, and the care in which the dishes are set around the table. Leonardo da Vinci knew this painting well, as he had visited it on numerous occasions. Da Vinci painted his own dramatic and globally famous version of "The Last Super" over 10 years later.

DA VINCI
1452 - 1519

- The most reproduced artist in history
- Wrote backwards: read his writings in a mirror
- THE Renaissance Man: GREAT at EVERYTHING

GIANTS ~ THE PEOPLE

Leonardo da Vinci's unmatched sense of curiosity and sheer raw intelligence has made him a true legend - even today, 500 years after his death.

Leonardo was born in the town of Vinci (just west of Florence), the illegitimate son of Piero Fruosino di Antonio, a notary. Being illegitimate, he was not allowed to take the name of his father, and so was simply called Leonardo da Vinci (Leonardo from Vinci).

Since early childhood, Leonardo showed an unquenchable sense of curiosity, imagination and creativity. He was fascinated by the workings of nature: how birds fly, why stars move, why the heart beats, etc. Everywhere he walked, he would stop to notice a flower blooming from a bud, or a frog growing from a tadpole. His questions were endless, and his curiosity was boundless.

 Portrait of a bearded da Vinci painted by Francesco Melzi

At the age of 13, he was admitted into one of Florence's premiere art workshops, led by the then famous Maestro Andrea del Verrocchio. Even as an apprentice, Leonardo showed an unusually great capacity for the arts. Once he was asked to paint an 'angel' in a Verrocchio project called "The Baptism of Christ" (pg 44). Verrocchio was so dumbstruck and intimidated by the sheer genius of his young student that he vowed never to pick up a brush again.

Leonardo moved around Italy at the behest of notable patrons such as the Duke Ludovico Sforza with whom da Vinci worked for nearly 18 years. Later, he acquired commissions from such notable patrons as Giuliano de' Medici, and the King of France, for whom he created such famous works of art as the Mona Lisa and the Last Supper.

At the age of 67 Leonardo died supposedly in the arms of the King of France, in the beautiful Loire Valley township of Amboise, although this belief has since been brought into question.

While in Florence however, da Vinci was well-known for the wide variety of his skills and of his unsquelchable curiosity.

The rivalry between the elder da Vinci and the younger and famously temperamental Michelangelo is legendary. It was Leonardo who attempted (unsuccessfully) to have Michelangelo's "David" placed in a niche high upon the Church of Santa Maria del Fiore so that it would not clutter the Piazza della Signoria. 🌼

 This sculpture of da Vinci stands majestically in the gallery of giants outside of the Uffizi Gallery.

LEONARDO DA VINCI

Polymath ◆ Scientist ◆ Cartographer ◆ Anatomist Engineer ◆ Mathematician ◆ Musician ◆ Painter Inventor ◆ Botanist ◆ Writer ◆ Hydro Mechanic

Da Vinci's Mysterious Lost Painting

Leonardo da Vinci and Michelangelo were both commissioned to cover the two great walls in the Salone dei Cinquecento (Hall of 500), inside the **Palazzo Vecchio**, with representations of famous (and victorious) Florentine battles. Da Vinci chose to depict a scene from

the "Battle of Anghiari," while Michelangelo selected to illustrate the "Battle of Cascina," which he never finished.

Stories are told locally that these two Giants would sometimes be known to 'show up for work' at the same time. Sometimes they would argue. Sometimes they would curse each other. And sometimes they were known to have gone days together without ever having spoken a single word to each other.

Leonardo's "Battle of Anghiari" was considered to be a masterpiece that outdid even his own "Last Supper." Wild war-horses and men were depicted in a gigantic tangle of limbs and hooves. But it remained in public for only 50 years, when the Palazzo Vecchio underwent a remodel. Giorgio Vasari was later hired to provide a painting to replace the original da Vinci work. Since the original painting has been lost, Peter Paul Ruben created this image based on a compilation of preparatory drawings left behind by Leonardo da Vinci.

Eureka!

Recently in 2012, art diagnostician Maurizio Seracini announced that he had found the original da Vinci fresco and that it was never removed or destroyed as previously thought, but that it was still there UNDERNEATH the Vasari painting where it has been hiding for over 500 years! This created a huge uproar

throughout the global art community and a team was brought in to examine the Vasari painting. But alas, the investigation was halted later that year due to conflicts with the parties involved.

Leonardo da Vinci

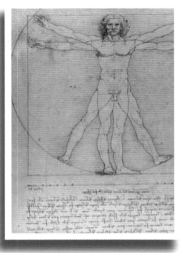

Vitruvian Man

 *This pen-and-ink drawing, created and made famous by da Vinci, depicts the perfect dimensions of the human body as described by the ancient Roman "Father of Architecture," Vitruvius. It is formally known as the "Canon of Proportions" or the "Proportions of Man." In it, Vitruvius described the fundamentals of the cosmic order.*

EXTRA: Regarding architecture, Vitruvius maintained three basic tenets of design: "All structures must be strong, functional and beautiful."

"Sfumato"

It was da Vinci that invented the 'sfumato' style of painting, which is the 'smoky' technique that makes distances fade away into the background. An excellent example of this can be seen clearly in his ultra-famous "Last Supper."

Possessing a life-long fascination with the principles of flight, da Vinci created seemingly endless drawings of a variety of flying machines, many of which wouldn't actually become built for centuries to come.

"The Last Supper" now hangs in the Convent of Santa Maria delle Grazie in Milan, Italy.

GIANTS ~ THE PEOPLE

The First Vegetarian?

Leonardo proved time and again to possess a great respect for all things living. For example, he was a vegetarian centuries before it became fashionable. He was known to purchase caged birds only to turn around and release them. This was partially due to his love for living creatures, but it also to helped him to solve one of the biggest puzzles in nature: flight. His bottomless sense of curiosity led him to ponder the inner workings of science and nature, and no topic escaped his attention. He studied cadavers to understand about sickness and about how the human body operates in general; he studied all things mechanical in order to solve problems like the building of bridges and dams, as well as military issues. His writing ran from right to left because he was left-handed. This made it easy to distinguish his strokes versus his teacher Verrocchio's strokes, as his were clearly made by a left-hander and Verrocchio was right-handed.

Did you Know?

The "Last Supper" and the "Mona Lisa" are the two most reproduced pieces of art in the world. They are rivaled only by Michelangelo's "Creation of Man" which was painted on the ceiling of the Sistine Chapel in Rome.

Secret Woman

In 1493 Leonardo, who was living in Milan at that time, was known to pay regular visits to a woman who went by the name of Catarina. In his tax documents, she is listed as one of his dependents. When she died in 1495, her funerary documents suggested that perhaps Leonardo was her son.

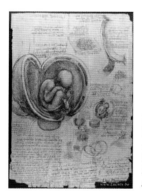

◀ *The large number of drawings and writings left behind by da Vinci illustrate his famous left-handed mirrored style of writing.*

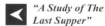
◀ *"A Study of The Last Supper"*
Da Vinci practiced sketching the apostles for his upcoming "Last Supper" project, a commission he received from the Convent of Santa Maria del Grazie in Milan. You can see that he wrote the names of each apostle above their heads in his famous left-handed backward penmanship.

GIANTS ~ THE PEOPLE

*Da Vinci began painting the **famous** "Mona Lisa" in Florence. It can now be seen in the Louvre in Paris, France.*

Leo's Job Search

The young da Vinci felt the pressure of massive competition to obtain work because of so many existing masters like **Andrea del Verrocchio, Sandro Botticelli** and **Fra Filippo Lippi,** among many others. So he pens a letter to the Duke of Milan extolling his own virtues and states why the duke should hire him as an artist. In this letter he lists his abilities as follows:

"I can build bridges
I can build weapons
I can build machines to break rocks
I can design buildings
I can manage water-flow for a city"

"And I can paint and sculpt as well as anyone else too."

"If any of the above-named things seem to anyone to be impossible or not feasible, I am most ready to make the experiment in your park, or in whatever place may please your Excellency - to whom I commend myself with the utmost humility."

Note: Since Giorgio Vasari was known to have used anecdotal information when he wrote his book *Lives of the Artists,* the identity of 'Lisa' has been refuted. Recently the portrait was said to be that of Lisa Gherardini - not Lisa Giocondo as previously thought. But was Gherardini her maiden name? Several theories still remain, but until this can be proven with a DNA analysis, the jury is still out.

THE PATIENCE OF MONA

Giorgio Vasari, in his *"Artists"* book, states that "Francesco del Giocondo, Leonardo created a portrait of his wife Lisa, famously entitled '**Mona Lisa**.' It is noted that during the four years it took to paint her, Leonardo had musicians brought in to sing to her and clowns to entertain her and to make her smile. This was a commonly used tactic, since, as in this case, it might take a VERY long time before a piece was completed.

SHE LIVES

"Anyone wishing to see the degree to which art can imitate Nature can easily understand this from the head, for here Leonardo reproduced all the details that can be painted with subtlety. The eyes have the lustre and moisture always seen in living people, while around them are the lashes and the reddish tones which cannot be produced without the greatest care. The eyebrows could not be more natural, for they represent the way the hair grows in the skin - thicker in some places and thinner in others, following the pores of the skin. The nose seems lifelike with its beautiful pink and tender nostrils. The mouth, with its opening joining the red of the lips to the flesh of the face, seemed to be real flesh rather than paint. Anyone who looked very attentively at the hollow of her throat would see her pulse beating: to tell the truth, it can be said that this portrait was painted in a way that would cause every brave artist to tremble and fear, whoever he might be."
-- *Giorgio Vasari,*
"The Lives of the Artists"

From "Cartoon" to Fresco in Four Easy Steps

The word 'cartoon' as we use it today defines line drawings that represent scenes of life in a more or less fantastical and or humorous way. In the Middle Ages, a 'cartoon' referred to the preparatory drawing that was created before a fresco (painting on wet plaster) was actually painted.

1. The artist would create a full-sized line drawing on a sheet of paper. This is the 'cartoon'.

2. Then he would go over every line in that cartoon pricking pin holes (using a pin or a pricking wheel) along all of the lines.

3. He would then paste the paper up on the wet-plastered wall intended for the finished fresco, and brush a light dusting of charcoal over the sheet. The charcoal that went through the pin holes left little black dots of dust on the blank wall.

4. After the sheet of paper was removed, the black dusty dotted outline of the cartoon appeared on the wall. To finish it off, the artist would fill in the lines with color and shading. Finito!

The da Vinci Codex is a 72-page document (18 sheets of paper, folded in half and written by hand on both sides) that speaks of the endless questions that crossed this Giant's mind, such as why fossils exist, where the moon's brightness comes from, the movement of water and erosion, tectonics, etc. His observations were astonishingly insightful, as he defined many aspects of nature and physics long before they were 'officially' discovered by later scientists.

GIANTS ~ THE PEOPLE

> *"da Vinci ...displayed infinite grace in everything he did."*
> *-Giorgio Vasari*

▲ *Fabric folds and draping make for an excellent study in light and shading.*

"In the normal course of events many men and women are born with various remarkable qualities and talents; but occasionally, in a way that transcends nature, a single person is marvelously endowed by heaven with beauty, grace and talent in such abundance that he leaves other men far behind. ...Everyone acknowledged that this was true of Leonardo da Vinci, an artist of outstanding physical beauty who displayed infinite grace in everything he did and who cultivated his genius so brilliantly that all problems he studied were solved with ease. He possessed great strength and dexterity; he was a man of regal spirit and tremendous breadth of mind..."
~Giorgio Vasari *"Lives of the Artists"*

Finding Leonardo Da Vinci Today

in Florence
Da Vinci Museum:
 - Via dei Servi, 66
Uffizi *(exterior sculpture)*
Santa Croce *(Tribute Tomb)*

in Italy
"**Leda**" *Galleria Borghese, Rome*
"**Vitruvian Man**" *Gallerie dell'Accademia, Venice, Italy*
"**The Last Supper**" *Church Santa Maria delle Grazie, Milan*
The Home of da Vinci *Anchiano, Tuscany*
Leonardo da Vinci Museum, *Vinci, Italy*

Internationale

"**Mona Lisa**"
   Musée du Louvre, Paris, France
"**Virgin of the Rocks**"
   - National Gallery, London, UK
"**Madonna of the Carnation**"
   - Alte Pinakothek, Munich, Germany
"**Madonna Litta**
   - Hermitage, St. Petersburg, Russia
"**Lady with an Ermine**"
   - Czartoryski Museum, Cracow, Poland

THE PEOPLE ~ GIANTS

SAVONAROLA
1452 - 1498

- A zealot monk intent on bringing back the Dark Ages
- Ignited the original Bonfire of the Vanities
- Was arrested, tortured, hung and burned by Church decree

During the reign of Lorenzo "il Magnifico" de' Medici, a Dominican Friar named Girolamo Savonarola strode into town wanting to express his feelings (loudly) that all of the 'free thinking' stuff and all of the nude statues and paintings were clearly the work of the devil. And to this, he gave credit (blame) to Lorenzo.

He started a campaign of followers and taught them to hate the Medici, and to reform themselves according to his personal edicts. With a rather theatrical approach, he professed a return to devout Christianity. He proclaimed that he had visions and heard messages that were sent directly from God, (hearing voices?) and in addition he proclaimed his own divinity saying that nothing can hurt him because of this personal relationship with God.

Girolamo Savonarola
by Fra Bartolomeo

Upon his deathbed, Lorenzo was concerned that perhaps some of his own decisions might not be approved by God, so he called Savonarola to hear his last 'Confession' so that he might be forgiven before he died. But because Savonarola was a dedicated nonsupporter of the Medici, Savonarola would have nothing of this, and he refused to hear the confession and to offer forgiveness to Lorenzo before he died. [Note: It is questionable whether this circumstance actually transpired. But this is the version of the story locals enjoy telling still today.]

A couple of years after Lorenzo's death, Savonarola had become successful in taking over the spiritual sensibilities of the general population of Florence, as well as civic leadership. He felt that his newly-found popularity entitled him to make changes toward cleaning up this filthy city. He decided that 'certain women' would be branded as whores and should be burned at the stake. He decided that homosexuality was a burnable offense, and that artists who made nude paintings and statues should be burned as well.

BONFIRE OF THE VANITIES
In February 1497 (five years after the death of Lorenzo the Magnificent), Savonarola created an opportunity for citizens to rid themselves of their evil creations & belongings by holding a public bonfire during the Mardi Gras festival. The idea was for people who owned 'stuff' to free themselves from the sins of materialism by throwing their worldly goods into the fire. 'Unacceptable' books were also to be thrown into the fire. Artists were to throw their shameful works into the fires as well.

GIANTS ~ THE PEOPLE

The many (nude) statues that stand in the Piazza dei Lanzi (in Piazza della Signoria) today will forever look down upon the Plaque which lies where Savonarola and his two most devout followers were ex-ecuted.

Fearful for their own souls, many people burned their belongings and their personal items of vanity such as nice clothes, mirrors, cosmetics, musical instruments, and even books including some famous written works by such authoritative greats as Boccaccio. Sadly, some of the great artists, such as Sandro Botticelli were known to have thrown some of their own exquisite works of art into what has since become known as the "Bonfire of the Vanities."

Because of mounting political differences with the Catholic Church, Savonarola was ordered to stop representing his eccentric preaching as being related to the Catholic Church. But onward he pushed, giving no notice to the barrage of warnings coming from the Vatican.

Eventually as his popularity waned, the people wanted him to prove his 'direct relationship with God' and the reality of his visions. The Church, weary of his on-going jabbering, had him arrested and thrown into a cell in the tower of the Palazzo Vecchio, where after threats of torture, he confessed that his representation as a special messenger from God was untrue. The angry Florentines decided that Savonarola should be sentenced to death. But because of their benevolence, he was hanged first, and then his body was burned in a bonfire right outside of the Palazzo Vecchio.

Today you will find in the Piazza della Signoria (in front of the Neptune water sculpture), a bronze plaque in the cobblestone where Savonarola's body was burned. The people of Florence have never forgotten their ill-conceived mistake of becoming so easily intoxicated by this purveyor of spiritual graffiti. 🌸

113

GIANTS ~ THE PEOPLE

The Execution of a "Mad Monk"

Girolamo Savonarola was hell-bent on cleaning up Dodge. Or in this case, Florence. He detested anything that represented wealth: jewelry, extra changes of clothing, more than one pair of shoes, and gambling. He detested comedy, jokes, a sense of humor, homosexuality - and sex in general. He detested music not related to religion, plays, poetry and laughter. He hated this plague that people have been calling 'art,' especially the nudity, the open sexuality, and the unrelenting displays of this 'art' in public. He detested the whole humanist movement that encouraged individuals to think for themselves, to be creative, and to explore their own curiosities.

But more than anything else, he hated the people he felt were responsible for this whole disgraceful "Up with People" movement: the Medici.

He could be seen preaching from a soapbox as comfortably and as loudly as from a pulpit that all of these horrifying excesses must be stopped or there will be a "Coming" that will destroy everyone. His seemingly endless and extremely vocal rants encouraged the people to turn against their 'beloved' Lorenzo. He held public bonfires where he encouraged folks to burn all of their (previously mentioned) excesses. These were later to become known at "The Bonfires of the Vanities". He fired off letters to the Pope in Rome pleading for some backup to assist him with the removal of the evil Lorenzo 'il Magnifico' de' Medici.

The premature death of Lorenzo (who died at age 43) in 1492 became Savonarola's best recruiting tool as he used this tragic circumstance as an illustration of God's punishment for the prior century of Medici-driven evil practices. He brandished threats that if the citizens did not jump on board with him and his inordinate beliefs, the death of their cherished leader was merely the beginning.

Several more years passed as this self-designated Prophet's rant became increasingly bombastic. In Rome the Pope finally concluded that continued support for Savonarola would eventually backfire on him and on the Papacy in general. After all, wasn't the current Pope, Alexander VI (Rodrigo Borgia), becoming the symbol of greed and excess himself? Perhaps it was time to put an end to all of this vocal gibberish that was coming from Florence. And so with a dismissive wave of his hand...

On Palm Sunday in the year 1498, representatives from Rome showed up on the doorstep of the Convent of San Marco, the residence of Savonarola, to place him under arrest. He and two other Friars, his most devout followers, were taken to a cell in the Palazzo Vecchio where he was imprisoned for approximately seven weeks. During his containment, Savonarola was brought to confessing that he was simply following the 'voices' of God that he heard every single day. *(Hearing voices? Hmm...)*

On May 23rd, the three monks were escorted out into the sunlight to the Piazza della Signoria, where a robust crowd of citizens, most of whom were anxious to witness the demise of Savonarola, stood in front of a platform. Over this platform, dangled three empty nooses, like expectant balloons waiting for the air that would give them purpose.

This painting by an anonymous artist hangs in the Gallery of San Marco as a reminder to Florentines of this tumultuous period in their history.

*A plaque can be found in the ground outside the front door of the Palazzo Vecchio. The Latin inscription translates roughly to "Here the Brothers Domenico Buonvicini and Sylvester Maruffi, on the 23 of May in 1498, hanged and burned with Brother Girolamo Savonarola. After four centuries **we remember**."*

The two devoted friars were the first to be tortured, then hanged until they died, then burned in a (wouldn't you know it?) BONFIRE. The executioner smiling at Savonarola gave him the look that so obviously said "Next." He was known to have asked Girolamo if he had any last statements, to which Savonarola responded, "The Lord suffered at least this much for me." (Is this last part really true? Nobody knows, but the locals really like including this in the story.)

NICCOLÒ MACHIAVELLI
1469 - 1527

- Father of Modern Political Theory
- Self-proclaimed enemy of the Medici family
- Diplomatic intermediary between Florence and the Vatican

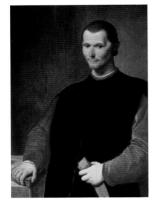

Niccolò di Bernardo dei Machiavelli was born in Florence in 1469, the same year that Lorenzo de' Medici came into power. Interestingly enough, his pro-Republic political views were diametrically opposed to the Medici way of doing 'business'.

As a child in a family of means, he was schooled in grammar and Latin. Few folks at that time possessed the ability to read and write, but because the printing press was well underway to producing a hailstorm of materials, the demand for 'readers' was far greater than the supply. This is what led to his career in the government.

The death of Lorenzo "il Magnifico" de' Medici in 1492 fed the fire of political upheaval for the next few decades to come. This was the perfect time for a quiet guy like Machiavelli, who opposed the Medici 'regime' to come into the spotlight.

Portrait of Niccolò Machiavelli by Santi di Tito

After Savonarola was executed in 1498 (*p114*), Machiavelli was appointed to the position of the keeper of the Official Florentine Government Documents for the renewed Republic. In addition he was appointed to the "Dieci di Libertà e Pace" (Ten of Liberty & Peace), the Ministers of War and the Interior. But seeing the brutal practices of the recent Pope Alexander VI (Rodrigo Borgia) and his son Cesare, who commonly used the Church as the excuse to bring most of central Italy under their power, Machiavelli made several ultimately unsuccessful trips to Rome to meet with the new Pope Julius II to use his diplomatic skills to find areas of commonality.

Eventually, Giovanni de' Medici who at this point was a favored Cardinal under Pope Julius II, used his relationship with the Pope to convince him to utilize the Spanish Army to subdue the Florence Republic and to place the Medici family back in power.

Machiavelli, believed that the best armies are those that are populated with local men who possess a vested love for their home land - rather than the unstable loyalties of a hired militia. He gathered people from in and around Florence to ward off the onslaught of the Pope. Whether they were armed with pitchforks, shovels or guns, they awaited the Pope's army. But very quickly, his citizen's army was wiped out in a bloodbath that resulted in the Medici retaking Florence, the renewed downfall of the Republic, and the arresting of Machiavelli by the new Medici enforcers.

While in prison under the charges of conspiracy against the Medici, Machiavelli endured harsh torture suffering two dislocated shoulders, all the while maintaining his innocence. After three weeks, he was released and exiled from his hometown of Florence. It was during this exile that he penned his famous book The Prince. Today, Machiavelli's book is still read globally to teach the 'Machiavellian' perspectives and their impact in political, social, and economic environments.

GIANTS ~ THE PEOPLE

Historian ◆ *Philosopher* ◆ *Diplomat*
Pacifist ◆ *Republican* ◆ *Playwrite* ◆ *Poet*
Humanist ◆ *Writer* ◆ *Musician*

THE PEOPLE ~ GIANTS

Is Machiavelli just Misunderstood?

The term "Machiavellian" is often misapplied to the man himself. Throughout his lifetime, he wrote many books. Of them, the best known today is "The Prince." He keenly observed that there are two types of leadership: Princedoms and Republics. In the still-popular"The Prince," he cynically outlines the traits and methodologies of the leaders of various Princedoms, most of whom practiced cruelty, cunning, deception and any-means-to-and-end as a way of Rule. The term "Machiavellian" speaks not to the man himself, but to his observations of cold-blooded leaders, and war strategies (good or bad). What many do not realize is that Machiavelli himself was a philosopher, a diplomat, a pacifist and a humanist. He loathed the techniques used by leaders that he felt were ruthless, such as the Borgias and some of the Medici, among others. Other works penned by Machiavelli include "The Art of War," "History of Florence," "Discourses on Livius," "Methods of the Duke Valentino," and satirical writings that include "La Mandragola" (The Mandrake).

Quotes from "The Prince"

"All the States and Governments by which men are or ever have been ruled, are either Republics or Princedoms. Of Republics I shall not now speak, having elsewhere spoken of them at length. Here I shall treat exclusively of Princedoms"
~ *The Prince: chapter i*

"He who has not first laid his foundations may be able with great ability to lay them afterwards, but they will be laid with trouble to the architect and danger to the building."
~ *The Prince: chapter vii*

Machiavelli's likeness forever ponders as it stands outside of the Uffizi Gallery.

NICCOLÒ MACCHIAVELLI

MICHELANGELO
1475 - 1564

- The epitome of The Artist and his Artistry
- Sculpted the globally cherished statue of "David"
- Painted the "Creation" on the ceiling of the Sistine Chapel
- The highest-paid artist in known history (up until his death)

When he was a child, Michelangelo Buonarroti was fascinated with stone. He loved to carve. His father and his uncles admonished him severely by beating him and telling him that "...sculpting was the basest of all careers" and that he should stop this sculpting business and stick to the respectable (and well-paying) job of 'lettering' or even of goldsmithing. But thankfully, these incidents only solidified the boy's steadfast drive toward drawing and sculpting. Michelangelo grew to become the most famous (and highest paid) artist in the world.

In Florence, Lorenzo de' Medici, a wealthy ruler and art lover, had a garden (art school) near the Church of Santa Croce where he paid the artistic Master Masaccio to teach young artists to paint and to sculpt. Masacchio found two young boys who showed exquisite talent, and so brought them into his garden. One of them was Michelangelo and the other was a

Michelangelo Buonarroti by Daniele da Volterra

young man named Pietro Torrigiano. One day, Lorenzo visited the garden when he picked up a crumpled scrap of paper from the floor. Seeing that it had incredible potential, he asked who was responsible for the drawing. He was told that a teenaged boy by the name Michelangelo drew it. Medici went to the boy and saw that he was working on a sculpture of a fully-toothed gargoyle. Lorenzo chuckled and said that gargoyles had fewer and more ugly teeth. After he left, Michelangelo, wanting nothing more than to please his Master, hit the statue with a hammer knocking out its teeth.

Inspired by the boy's raw genius at such a young age, Lorenzo de' Medici contacted the father of the boy and agreed to pay him if he allowed the boy to stay and be raised by the Medici family and schooled professionally. And so it was that Michelangelo spent his teen years in the house of Medici.

Leaving his Mark
Michelangelo was known to have spent weeks selecting the perfect piece of stone. Once found, he would sketch the piece, complete with its natural lines and striations. This way he would know that the correct stone was delivered when it arrived to him several months later.

Making of a Maestro
Michelangelo spent the next several years in the Medici household, where he was treated as though he were another Medici child. He was allowed to freely explore his imagination and to test his abilities by experimenting with a variety of media. Although he demonstrated great promise in several of them - especially drawing and painting - he felt the strongest pull toward the toughest of them all: sculpting from stone.

Sculptor ◆ Architect ◆ Painter Poet ◆ Engineer

Punching Michelangelo

Michelangelo's unfailing reputation for having an ill temper is legendary. Even in his youth, he was known to often provoke anger. So it goes that one day while in art school in the beautiful garden of Lorenzo de' Medici, he said something to anger a fellow young artist. This artist, Pietro Torrigiano, was so incensed by Michelangelo's insult that he hauled off and punched him square in the nose so hard that Cellini quoted Torrigiano as saying "I felt bone and cartilage go down like a biscuit beneath my knuckles." For this, Torrigiano was banished from Florence by Lorenzo de' Medici. But the question that hung in the air since that time was whether or not Michelangelo had learned from this incident to keep his insults inside.
(Not a chance! But then again, we wouldn't want to change a single thing about this rare genius.)

When Michelangelo included his own likeness within his works, he often despaired at the ugliness of his hideously crooked broken nose. Above is his famed Florence Pietà "The Deposition," in which he substituted his own face in the place of Nicodemus.

During some evenings, the young Michelangelo was allowed to sit quietly and unobtrusively in the parlor as the elite, educated gentlemen of the city would visit to drink a sweet liqueur and discuss the issues of the city and the world. One of the more popular topics was the one that intrigued Michelangelo so much that it had a colossal effect on his art for the rest of his life. Those were the stories of the ancient Greeks and the Roman empire.

Through those stories, he came to understand that over 1,000 years before, there existed giant cultures that lived a life so vastly different than the one he had always known. There was mathematics and literature (what in the heck were those?!?) and scientific experiments and philosophies that collided with everything that he had been taught. The music and the performing arts were boundless. But more important than anything else to our young Michelangelo: there was a vast array of art - everywhere!

But not just paintings and sculptures that tell the stories of the bible, those that were created to live inside the walls of the churches, or those stories of just one God. He was seeing art that told wild stories of a whole hoard of gods! There was Bacchus, the god of wine. And a god named Apollo who was the god of truth and prophecy. And Diana the goddess of the hunt. There was the god of love that the Greeks called Eros and that the Romans called Cupid. And the list went on and on. There was a god or goddess that controlled pretty much everything.

GIANTS ~ THE PEOPLE

The stories that went along with these gods were mystifying and altogether fantastic to the ears of our young Michelangelo, as he sat in silence, listening as these ancient stories unfolded before him. The images created in his mind were strange, and foreign and provocative. "So," he began asking himself, "What if I carved something from one of those ancient stories instead of the standard biblical stories that all of the other guys have been carving for the past centuries?" His mind flooded with images and scenes and people and stories that began to permeate all of his thoughts, his dreams at night, his very soul. And all he wanted was for the world to get out of his way so that he could release these images from inside his head.

Greatness Set Loose Upon the World

When Michelangelo was 19, his beloved Master Lorenzo de' Medici passed away and left him distraught and unemployed. At that time, the city of Florence was in turmoil as rival factions vied to fill the empty seat of supremacy left vacant by the death of Lorenzo. Girolamo Savonarola, a Dominican monk with a fire-and-brimstone style of preaching, had mustered a large following that believed the city had strayed too far from the church with all of this 'free thinking' stuff and nude art everywhere. He blamed Lorenzo de' Medici for this and managed to split the city in half over this issue.

Confused and grieving, Michelangelo left Florence to escape the "Bonfires" into which artists were required, at the threat of eternal damnation by Savonarola, to throw their art for fiery destruction. Michelangelo went to Rome where he found work as a sculptor and a painter.

In 1499, Michelangelo was hired by a French Cardinal to carve the Pietà: Mary cradling her dead son. He personally went to the quarry in the town of Carrara to supervise the cutting and transportation of the marble. Upon its completion, the Pietà was hailed as a masterpiece. But this was not enough for the temperamental artist. He needed to find a project that would not just make him famous in his lifetime; he wanted eternal fame.

Periodically, he would return to Florence to visit his father and to complete a variety of projects, one of which was the tomb for his beloved patron Lorenzo de' Medici and his brother Giovanni de' Medici. Today these tombs can be found the the Cappella Medici (the Medici Chapel inside the Basilica di San Lorenzo).

He accepted commissions for projects all over Tuscany and down into Rome. They were all nice, but still he searched for the one single project that would once and for all, separate him from the hoards of hacks who dared to call themselves artists. And so he found one, when he learned that the Church elders wanted a statue from the biblical story of "David and Goliath" to be sculpted for the top of the Church of Santa Maria del Fiore...!

And if that weren't enough, as surely it was, he later proceeded to Rome where he created what was to become one of the most reproduced paintings in all of history: the ceiling of the Vatican's Sistine Chapel. And the rest, as they say, is history.

Michelangelo died in Rome at the age of 88. He had previously made it clear that he wished to be entombed in the Church of Santa Croce, which is where you will find his tomb today.

Eww, Those Feet!

After Michelangelo died, the mortician had to carefully peel the boots from Michelangelo's legs and feet. This was due to the fact that Michelangelo had not removed the boots for an unknown number of years, and the skin had grown to the leather in various places.

THE PEOPLE ~ GIANTS

The Sleeping Cupid

When he was 19 years old, Michelangelo learned quickly that patrons were becoming less interested in works of art made by contemporary artists. Tastes had changed, as art buyers were becoming more interested in the 'Ancient Art' that came from ancient Rome and Greece.

He had just finished carving a beautiful little "Sleeping Cupid" when he learned of these preferences. Not knowing from where his next paycheck would come, he rubbed the Cupid with an acidic mud and buried it. When he dug it up a few months later, it appeared to be an 'ancient' piece of art, withall the appropriate microbial 'stuff' growing all over it.

He sold it to an art dealer who specialized in ancient art, and he eventually sold it to Cardinal di San Giorgio, Raffaele Riario. Riario, a man known for his spontaneous acts of cruelty, realized it was a fake, and so ordered his men to go into the forest and find this Michelangelo fellow and "bring him to me." Riario considered having Michelangelo gutted, but since he clearly recognized the talent in the young artist's work, he decided to give him another chance.

When asked why he never married,

Michelangelo replied, "I have too much of a wife in this art that has always afflicted me, and the works I shall leave behind will be my children, and even if they are nothing, they will live for a long while." ~ Smithsonian.com

Few people are aware that in addition to being an artist, an architect and a sculptor, Michelangelo was also an accomplished poet, having written over 300 poems. It is said that in this "Doom of Beauty" he writes of his friend Tommaso dei Cavalieri, whose perfect beauty so entranced Michelangelo. But true beauty, like all things, fades. Today we find so many tributes to Cavalieri not only in Michelangelo's poetry, but in his sculptures and paintings as well.

Michelangelo The Poet

His temperamental nature left Michelangelo dispossessed of meaningful relationships throughout his life, save a very few. One such was with his friend Tommaso Cavalieri. Michelangelo loved to sculpt the body of his beautiful Tommaso, and wrote many poems in tribute to him.

"Doom of Beauty"
by Michelangelo Buonarotti

Choice soul, in whom,
as in a glass, we see,
Mirrored in thy pure form
and delicate,
What beauties heaven
and nature can create,
The paragon of
all their works to be!
Fair soul, in whom love,
pity, piety,
Have found a home,
as from thy outward state
We clearly read,
and are so rare and great
That they adorn
none other like to thee!
Love takes me captive,
beauty binds my soul,
Pity and mercy
with their gentle eyes
Wake in my heart
a hope that cannot cheat.
What law, what destiny,
what fell control,
What cruelty,
or late or soon, denies
That death should spare
perfection so complete?

The 'Drunken' Bacchus

Cardinal Raffaele Riario decided that in repentance for creating that fake 'antique' Cupid sculpture, he would allow Michelangelo to create a sculpture that would reside in his famous sculpture garden. Being a huge admirer of Michelangelo's style of sculpture - and considering himself to be an educated connoisseur of great art - he granted Michelangelo the freedom to select the 'theme' of this piece that was to be unveiled in the coming Spring at an important social function. Michelangelo, who had unsatisfactory past dealings with Riario, set to work in secrecy. He decided to sculpt a new version of 'Bacchus' the Greek god of harvest - and the symbol of wine - with his satyr. When it was unveiled, the Cardinal was aghast when he saw an obviously drunken Bacchus with an oddly androgynous body. Once the crowd stopped laughing, the humiliated Cardinal confronted Michelangelo as to the meaning of such a work of bad taste, to which Michelangelo remarked simply that this could be no fault of his own because the piece of stone that Riario had purchased was flawed, and as a result, this was the figure that was trapped inside. "Never again will I EVER work with a flawed piece of stone!" he cried, leaving Riario to ponder quietly the wisdom of torture as it related to the impudent Michelangelo.

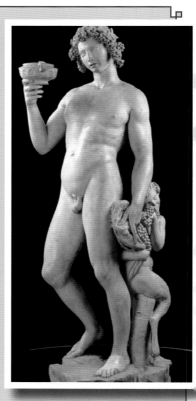

Secret Hideaway

Although Michelangelo was adopted in his youth by **Lorenzo 'il Magnifico' de' Medici**, decades later, in 1530, he found himself at odds with a different Medici: Pope Clement VII, Lorenzo's nephew Giulio de' Medici. Michelangelo was appointed as head man to bolster the fortifications around Florence, thereby fending the Pope's army off of the city. Alas, Giulio's side prevailed, and Florence surrendered. Michelangelo fled from the consequences of choosing the wrong side, and hid in a secret chamber beneath the Medici Chapel in the Basilica de San Lorenzo. This room, a mere 23' x 6.5', is where Michelangelo lived/hid for 3 months. While in there, he occupied his mind by sketching on the walls. Eventually, the Pope announced that Michelangelo be forgiven if he would agree to finish his work on the Medici tombs in the New Sacristy. The hidden chamber, and its masterful drawings, were only recently discovered in 1975.
(Read more on p191)

TOMB OF POPE JULIUS II

Michelangelo was called to Rome in 1505 when Pope Julius came upon the idea of having a memorial made for himself. He wished for Michelangelo to create for him the largest and most grandiose tomb ever seen. Michelangelo sketched out a rendering of the perfect tomb that consisted of forty separate statues with Moses as the central character. It also included six slaves: two of which currently reside in the Louvre, and four in the Accademia in Florence - in front of Michelangelo's beloved statue of "**David.**"

However, a number of conflicts arose during its creation that forced Michelangelo to stop work in the middle of its progress. Some of these conflicts are said to originate in jealousy from the architect "Bramante" (Michelangelo was quite vocal about the flaws in Bramante's work) who convinced the Pope that it was bad luck to create a tomb before you are dead. And from a younger **Raphael da Urbino** who convinced the Pope to recast Michelangelo into the role of a painter. Feeling that Michelangelo, who had never worked with color before, would prove that Raphael was a better painter than he, Raphael went so far as to suggest that for a project, Michelangelo could paint the ceiling of the Sistine Chapel. The Pope loved the idea. Michelangelo, a sculptor to the bone, felt that painting was beneath his talents. Nevertheless, he showed everyone who the grand master really was when he created on the chapel ceiling "**The Creation**" and later "**The Resurrection**" behind the altar within the same chapel.

The tomb, however remained unfinished until Michelangelo had completed the Sistine Chapel (1512), at which point he resumed and sculpted two of the Slaves and Moses. Upon the death of Julius II in 1513, the new Papal 'administration' drew up a new contract to change the original free-standing tomb to a wall-mounted structure. As the 'powers that be' changed over the next couple of decades, new contracts continued to change the structure. The final Tomb, much smaller and less ambitious than Michelangelo had planned, was finally completed in 1545 ~ after 40 years. Some of the statues that exist on the tomb today were (obviously) not created by Michelangelo himself.

Body Snatching

Michelangelo suffered many years with kidney stones, from which he may have died in 1564. After his death, he was buried in Rome. However, the Florentines knew of his wishes to be buried in his beloved Florence. Funded by Florentines, a pair of thieves went to Rome to steal Michelangelo's body and bring it to Florence for a proper burial. The two thieves located body, and hid it under some hay in their oxcart for transportation back to Florence. After this successful effort, Michelangelo's body was carefully interred in the Church of Santa Croce where you will find his tomb today.

Dead Man's Quarry

The process of cutting and transporting stone from a quarry was so difficult that a man was lost almost every time large hunks of stone were ordered.

123

GIANTS ~ THE PEOPLE

▲ *Michelangelo was commissioned to design the Cappella di Medici (The Medici Chapel) for his beloved patron and friend Lorenzo the Magnificent. The tomb of Lorenzo (left) is protected by the two statues representing 'Dusk & Dawn', and his brother Giuliano's tomb sits across the room being presided over by the two statues of 'Day & Night' (right). Adjacent to the Chapel is the Laurentian Library which was a feat of design brilliance by Michelangelo.*

Cadavers at Home

Michelangelo, intrigued with the inner workings of the human body, acquired corpses in order to study the anatomy and to understand what is underneath the skin that makes our bodies look the way they do. Living in a free room at the Church of Santo Spirito, he had the cadavers delivered there. Rumors flew around the city that he was actually murdering some of these poor people in order to carve them apart in that disgusting little room of his. But those accusations were never proven, and so ultimately disappeared. And to thank the prior for the free room (and for not complaining about the smell), Michelangelo carved a wooden crucifix for that church, which can still be seen in Santo Spirito today.

Florence "Pietà"

Michelangelo was in his mid-70's when he began carving the poignant "Florence Pietà" (right). He is thought to have created it for his own tomb in Santa Croce, but eight years into this project, Michelangelo found a flaw in the stone that he could not work with. So he threw his hammer at it in frustration, and refused to finish it. He later gave the sculpture to Antonio, his favored servant, who in turn brought in one of Michelangelo's students, Tiberio Calcagni, to finish the piece. Calcagni completed the Mary Magdalene portion (the lady on the left), although it differs greatly from Michelangelo's own great style. Calcagni died before being able to do any further damage to this piece.

The Altar That Didn't Quite Get There

After the prior incidents with Michelangelo, Cardinal Raffaele Riario understood that the better the artist, the more patience one must exercise in their dealings with them. He decided to give Michelangelo one more chance. Once again, he ordered his men to go into the forest and bring Michelangelo back to Rome. He ordered Michelangelo to carve an altarpiece for one of the chapels. Michelangelo scoffed that he would not sculpt from another flawed piece of stone provided by the Cardinal again. So Riario gave enough money to Michelangelo so that he could travel to the quarry in the town of Carrara to select the stone of his own choosing. And so, off he went.

But instead of purchasing the stone, Michelangelo took the money and with it, he bought a farm.

After some months had passed without yet seeing the altarpiece for which Riario had previously paid, he once again sent his men to bring Michelangelo back to Rome.

Riario asked Michelangelo, "Where is my stone? Where is my tomb? Where is my money?!?" to which Michelangelo replied, "Do you remember hearing about that boat that sank a few months ago carrying all that stone aboard? Well, your marble was on that boat!"

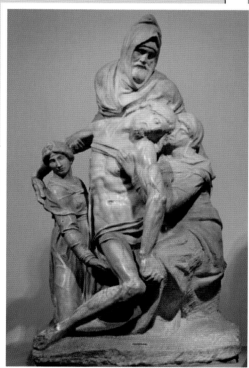

*Known as "The Deposition" and **"The Florence Pietà"** Nicodemus, Mary Magdalene and the Virgin Mary attempt to support the weight of the body of Christ as he was taken down from the cross. Note Michelangelo's skill at making something look really heavy. Representing weight is difficult with every medium, but most difficult with stone. Enjoy this magnificent piece in the Duomo Museum.*

Although the man here is supposed to represent Nicodemus (formally Joseph of Arimathea) it is evident that his all-too-familiar features are those of Michelangelo himself.

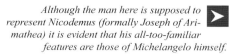

The 'David' Event

One day, Michelangelo heard that the church of Santa Maria del Fiore had a slab of marble that they wanted sculpted into a "David." And they wanted it to be placed in a niche high up on the outside of the church. Two other sculptors had started this project, but because of the limiting dimensions of the slab, they failed. The block was an awkward 17-feet tall, and far too thin to build a David that would be big enough to be seen so high up. Michelangelo rose to the challenge and began sculpting that block of stone in secret.

When it was finished, the town rejoiced in awe, so the proud Michelangelo decided that instead of putting it high up in the niche, it should be placed at ground level outside of the city hall (Palazzo Vecchio). Many of the citizens agreed. The general consensus was that if it was placed high upon the church, it would not get the notice that it deserved, and it would become a religious symbol. If placed at ground-level in front of a government building, people could admire it in all of its glorious detail, and it would become a civic symbol - a symbol of the people rather than one of the Church.

Leonardo da Vinci, not to be over-shadowed by Michelangelo, led the fight to put the statue high up on the church. But the city officials had the final word. David was put in the Piazza della Signoria in front of the Palazzo Vecchio where it stood for 350 years. Today David stands protected inside the Accademia, and a replica stands in its original place outside of the Palazzo Vecchio.

David has come to symbolize the city of Florence: Right vs Might, or Size Does Not Matter.

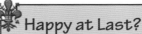

Happy at Last?

Upon the completion of his "David," Michelangelo was content knowing that he had separated himself from the growing rabble that so brazenly called themselves artists. NOT. Michelangelo was not known to be content with anything at any time. He continued dealing with the demons in his head that drove him to relentlessly push himself past all known limits in everything he did.

Herein lies the essence of his greatness.

Moving David

Upon the completion of the "David," men moved the 'Giant' from the Duomo to the Piazza della Signoria, less than one mile away. They laid down logs side-by-side, laid a large plank onto the logs, then laid the statue onto the plank. As they gently rolled this configuration forward, a log was left in the rear. A few men would run that log to the front of the rolling procession, and continue in this manner to its final destination. Along the way, they had to widen streets and disassemble bridges. It took four days to complete the move successfully. All-the-while Michelangelo accompanied the procession screaming, biting his nails and sweating profusely.

Today, this replica of "David" can be enjoyed at your leisure in the open air outside of the Palazzo Vecchio.

Skinny David

It is apparent from the side, just how THIN that block of marble really was. "David" was carved from a single piece of stone, and there was very little waste. In fact, on the top of his head and at the base, Michelangelo left the roughness of the outer edges of the original stone block, making it easy to see that David's dimensions stretch to the very edges of the original slab.

David was originally supposed to be put in a little niche high up in the church. Had this happened, it would have disappeared into religious obscurity and the world would not have had their beloved David to admire for all time to come.

GEMS ~ PLACES

1440's

DAVID
by Donatello

1473-1475

DAVID
by Verrocchio

Donatello's bronze statue of David, created in the 1440s, was the first of the three most important Davids. It is lauded as the first unsupported standing work of bronze cast during the Renaissance, and the first free-standing nude male sculpture made since antiquity. It depicts David, just after he defeated the giant, posed with his foot on Goliath's severed head. The boy is completely naked, apart from a laurel-topped hat and boots, and he is bearing the sword of victory.

Andrea del Verrocchio's bronze statue of David, the second of these three famous Davids, was created in the mid-1470s. It was commissioned by the Medici family, and it is claimed that Verrocchio modeled the statue after a handsome pupil in his workshop: the young Leonardo da Vinci. The statue represents the youthful David, future king of the Israelites, triumphantly posing over the head of the slain Goliath. *Note: It has since been proven that Verrocchio had intended for Goliath's head to be placed outside of David's left foot instead of between his feet as it is in Donatello's David.*

Both of these "Davids" can be found in The Bargello Museum.

DAVID
by Michelangelo
1501-1504

When Michelangelo received the commission to create a "David" statue, there were already two other very famous David's in Florence. Michelangelo found two main issues to ponder: One being how to create something of substance from this twice-damaged, too-slender piece of 17-foot tall stone, and the other was how to create a David that would be vastly different - and better, of course - than those *'other'* two Davids. After once again reading the famous story about David and Goliath, he felt that the most poignant moment in the story did not occur AFTER David slew Goliath, but in that single moment just BEFORE he cast his lethal stone. He felt that David was a strong and handsome young man who's inexperience in life possessed a mash-up of conflicting emotions: insecurity with courage, fear with anger, vulnerability with confidence, and defiance alongside innocence.

Michelangelo's ability to capture the collision of these strongly conflicting emotions through David's furrowed eyes has never since been equalled.

This is the defining moment that young David turned from a boy into a man.

David is staring earnestly and directly into the eyes of his foe Goliath. If you look at his sideways stance, the true thinness of the stone becomes startlingly apparent.

Unlike the other two Davids that the other artists portrayed the moment AFTER killing Goliath, Michelangelo's conception of David occurs in that single moment just BEFORE he cast his lethal rock.

Some things that you won't see until you walk around behind David: the sling that will hold the deadly stone is wrapped diagonally across his back. You can also see that the deadly stone is ready in his hand - which too, is invisible from the front.

This original "David" can be found in The Accademia.

GIANTS ~ THE PEOPLE

Finding Michelangelo Today

🌸 First and foremost, the Galleria dell'Accademia is where you will find the most famous sculpture in the world: Michelangelo's "David." Michelangelo's "Slaves" (originlly created for the Tomb of Pope Julius II) can be seen in the Accademia as well.

🌸 Outside of the Palazzo Vecchio you will see a copy of "David." Inside this Palazzo, you will find Michelangelo's sculpture "Genius of Victory" in the Hall of 500. This is also where he covered one of the great walls with his painting of the "Battle of Cascina". This painting was lost when Giorgio Vasari remodelled the Palazzo.

🌸 The Capella di Medici (the Medici Chapel) demonstrates Michelangelo's architectural prowess. Take the tour through the Chapel to see the Tombs of Lorenzo, his brother Giuliano, and many other members of the Medici family.

🌸 The Laurentian Library, designed by Michelangelo, was created for Lorenzo de' Medici. Note the creative staircase leading into the library: he ingeniously stacked ovals upon each other to from the visually-engaging steps.

🌸 During your visit to the Uffizi Gallery, go to Hall 35 where you will see Michelangelo's only surviving painting in Florence, the "Tondo Doni".

🌸 Casa Buonarotti, Michelangelo's House is a small museum that houses several of his sculptures and drawings.

🌸 In the Bargello, you will find Michelangelo's "Drunken Bacchus" sculpture, as well as his "Apollo," "Brutus," and the "Virgin Mother with the Baby Jesus" sculptures.

🌸 In the Museo dell'Opera del Duomo (the Duomo Museum), you will see Michelangelo's "Deposition" where he put his own face in the place of Nicodemus.

🌸 The Piazzale Michelangelo is the best spot in the city to enjoy the sunset. A replica of "David" stands tall and proud to keep you company.

🌸 ## In Italy
Milan, Sienna, Rome, Vatican City, Bologna

🌸 ## In the World
Bruges, Belgium; London & Oxford, England; Paris &, Chantilly & Mont Pellier, France; Haarlem, Netherlands; Boston & Fort Worth, US, and in St. Petersburg, Russia.

🌸 Bonus: In the city of Las Vegas, inside the Caesar's Palace Hotel, you will find a beautiful full-sized 9-ton reproduction of "David."

Can you find this Hidden Face?

At the front entrance of the Palazzo Vecchio, look down to the right. You will see this carving of a man attributed to Michelangelo. Some of the myths connected to it say that someone once bet Michelangelo that he couldn't carve a portrait with his hands tied behind his back (apparently Michelangelo won the bet); another states that there was a man who used to hang around outside the Palazzo talking incessantly. It is said that Michelangelo carved the likeness of that man into the wall to help alleviate his own boredom while the man talked and talked and talked.

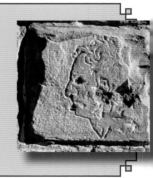

MICHELANGELO'S GREATEST WORKS IN ROME

Michelangelo's "Creation" is a cherished centerpiece in Rome's Sistine Chapel. His ability to depict his knowledge of the human body into his works of art is one of the most important reasons that Michelangelo's works have been so coveted for 500 years.

Little Known Secret
This is Michelangelo's famous "Last Judgment," a fresco painted onto the altar wall of the Sistine Chapel in the Vatican. Within the figure of St. Bartholomew, the martyr who was flayed alive, is a tragic and anguished self-portrait. He depicted his own face in the empty envelope of skin that hangs grotesquely from the saint's hand, a metaphor perhaps, for the artist's tortured soul?

> "Carving is easy. You just go down to the skin and stop."
>
> ~ Michelangelo Buonarotti

The Rome Pietà (1498) was young Michelangelo's first really famous sculpture created after he moved to Rome. When this piece was unveiled, it was celebrated as the greatest sculpture in the known world. And he was lauded as not only being the greatest sculptor in the world, but perhaps he was even greater than those great Roman masters of the ancient world. This Pietà can be seen today in St. Peter's Basilica in Vatican City.

THE PEOPLE ~ GIANTS

RAPHAEL
1483 - 1520

- The most prolific great artist in history
- Popular Ladies' Man
- Died on his 37th birthday
- The 'High Renaissance' ended upon his death

He was known by many names: Raffaello Santi, Raffaello de Urbino, Rafael Sanzio da Urbino, and just plain Raphael. Little was known about his early life, because written evidence such as personal letters or journals have never been produced. This has led many a historian to speculate about his life. Born in Urbino, Italy he was schooled in the well-established and famous school of the arts in Florence. In addition, he was also known as a draftsman and an architect. Inheriting his talents and sensitivities from his father, who was an artist and a poet, and his mother who was schooled in both visual arts as well as music, Raphael learned his famously good manners from being brought up in the world of the court where his parents often worked.

His rare and cherished talents as a painter covered a wide gamut of media, such as canvas, frescoes and tapestries. He was commonly commissioned to paint portraits of the rich and famous, from Lorenzo de' Medici to a variety of popes.

This "Raphael ~ a Self Portrait" can be found in the Uffizi Gallery

While in Rome, Raphael was appointed as 'Prefect' over all archaeological antiquities relating to ancient Rome that were being discovered all around the city. Wishing to create a visual survey in an attempt to organize this large variety of discoveries, he asked Pope Leo X (Giovanni di Lorenzo de' Medici) to halt the destruction of the old Roman monuments so this could be done. But the Pope wanted to see the new construction of St. Peter's Basilica, because its completion would help assuage some non-related financial 'issues.'

Raphael's works in Rome are still well-known today, as are the mysteries that surrounded his life. No jottings, not even doodles on scraps, have ever been found written in his hand. This lack of documentation has created many legends and even cults that were all created around the mysterious life - and abruptly premature death - of this most prolific artist. His tragic death represented the end of the 'High Renaissance' period. ✿

RAPHAEL'S POSITION IN THE RENAISSANCE

Thirsting to learn from the Florentine greats such as da Vinci and Michelangelo, Raphael moved to Florence shortly after his 21st birthday. At that point, da Vinci was at the height of his career as was Michelangelo. Raphael proceeded to copy (as was - and still is - a common learning practice) the most important works by both da Vinci and Michelangelo as well. Michelangelo at this point had already amassed a healthy hatred for the elder da Vinci. And when the clearly gifted talents of Raphael began to appear around town, Michelangelo found room in his heart to hate him too.

Raphael's generally-known style of painting clearly acknowledges his early apprenticeship under the master Perugino. Perugino was known for the 'clarity' in his work, and Raphael took that

Painter ◆ Architect ◆ Draftsman

▲ *(Left) The Sistine Madonna, (Center) La Crocefissione, (right) La Fornarina all demonstrate Raphael's recognizable style of 'clarity,' which was initially gleaned from Perugino who apprenticed Raphael as a child.*

Some say that Raphael may have somehow known that he was to live a very short life. They say that this is proven by the unusually extensive number of works that he created during his brief time on Earth,

concept of 'clarity' to new heights, adding his own interpretations of what he had learned from the Florentine masters Leonardo da Vinci and Michelangelo.

A common definition of the 'High Renaissance period' was punctuated by the trilogy of da Vinci, Michelangelo and Raphael. Some feel that the High Renaissance was completed upon the death of Raphael in 1520. Even though he was not born in nor did he die in Florence, he is never-the-less considered to be the end-point of the Florentine High Renaissance because of the deep influences of the masters and how Raphael in turn combined those influences into his own masterful and never-to-be-forgotten works.

RAPHAEL THE ARCHITECT

As a personal friend of the esteemed architect Donato Bramante, Raphael studied architecture with a fervor to match style of the known master architect. Upon Bramante's death, the commission to build the new St. Peter's Basilica in Rome was given to Raphael. Unfortunately, much of his contribution there - as well as his other architectural accomplishments - have been lost, altered or destroyed. Pope Julius II was in the midst of a restructuring of some of the streets and alleys in the city, which he envisioned a number of beautiful new buildings and structures to eventually live on these streets. Raphael is known to have designed the Palazzo Branconio dell'Aquila, the Chigi Chapel in the Villa Farnesina, Palazzo di Jacobo da Brescia, and the Villa Madama for Giulio de' Medici which is said to be the most sophisticated villa to date and had a great influence over architectural design from that point forward.

THE PEOPLE ~ GIANTS

"School of Athens" - *by Raphael*
fresco, 1509-1511 (Stanza della Segnatura, Palazzi Pontifici, Vatican City)

Socrates

Apollo

Plato
(Represented by Leonardo da Vinci)

Aristotle

Zoroaster

Epicuras

Alexander
the Great

Athena

Raphael

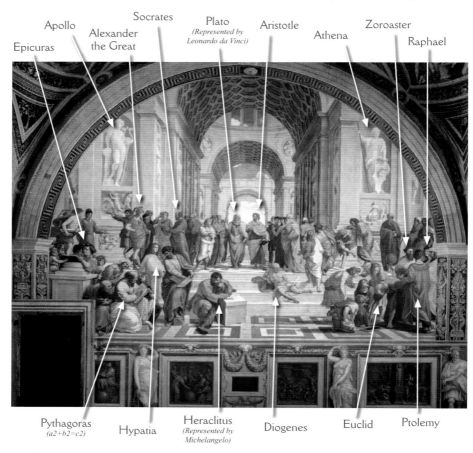

Pythagoras
(a2+b2=c2)

Hypatia

Heraclitus
(Represented by Michelangelo)

Diogenes

Euclid

Ptolemy

Created in 1511 at the behest of Pope Julius II, Raphael's "School of Athens" attempts to reconcile Philosophy, Astrology, Geometry and Poetry with Theology by depicting the most famous names from ancient Greece. Although the foreground is characteristic of Greek architecture, the main hall and the background hall seem to questioningly depict a more Romanesque architectural style. This fresco measures 25.5 feet in width.

Skull Worship

In the early 1700's, Raphael's skull was removed from its skeleton and displayed in the Accademia di San Luca in Rome where new art students would place their pencils upon it for inspiration. Even Goethe, who admired its "perfect brain-pan" had a cast of the skull made so that he could take it home and admire it daily. This practice of "Skull Worship" was maintained until 1833 when Raphael's tomb was opened and the skeleton was found completely intact, complete with skull.

(So the question remains: whose skull was actually being worshiped?)

"The liberality with which Heaven can unite in one person the inexhaustible riches of its treasures which are usually shared among many over a long period is seen in Raphael Sanzio of Urbino, who was as excellent as gracious, and endowed with a natural modesty and goodness sometimes seen in those who possess to an unusual degree a humane and gentle nature adorned with affability and good-fellowship, and he always showed himself sweet and pleasant with persons of every degree and in all circumstances. Thus Nature created Michelangelo Buonarroti to excel and conquer in art, but Raphael to excel in art and in manners also. In Raphael the rarest gifts were combined with such grace, diligence, beauty, modesty and good character that they would have sufficed to cover the ugliest vice and the worst blemishes. We may indeed say that those who possess such gifts as Raphael are not mere men, but rather mortal gods, and that those who by their works leave an honored name among us on the roll of fame may hope to receive a fitting reward in heaven for their labors and their merits."

Giorgio Vasari ~ *Lives of the Artists*

The "Wedding of the Virgin" was Raphael's most sophisticated altarpiece of this period.

THE TWO FACES OF RAPHAEL

Raphael's gentle handsomeness is well documented from his own hand. In existence today are several self-portraits where some admirers have been quoted as saying that Raphael's beautifully defined facial features are so perfect they resemble those perfect features known of Jesus Christ.

To match his perfect appearance was his reputation as a patient and even-handed boss. His workshop produced a highly unusual number of art pieces, as he utilized the talents of many artists to accommodate the wide variety of eager patrons who wanted to maintain their 'chicness' by possessing some of his artwork. The 'delicate' temperaments of many of his artists often clashed with the fustian dispositions of many a patron, which caused a commonly seen number of riffs between them. Raphael's good manners and ability to sooth both sides produced a working environment that many knew to be of a calmer nature than some of 'those other' studios.

It appeared that there was also another side to this well-heeled gentle man. His reputation as a womanizer was legendary. His friend, Cardinal Bernardo Bibbiena, talked Raphael into proposing to the Cardinal's niece Maria Bibbiena. However, once done, Raphael had second thoughts and was less than eager about this engagement and proceeded down a path of continuous affairs. His romps became well known, as was his favorite relationship with the daughter of a 'fornaro' (baker) by the name of Margherita Luti, who became known simply as his 'fornarina'. And it was after one rumbustious night with his fornarina that Raphael fell ill. Being too embarrassed to tell his doctors about that raucous night, it is said that he was misdiagnosed, given the wrong treatments, and tragically passed away within three weeks. He was only 37 years old. Upon his death, the Pope wept grievously and publicly, and made it known that his sadness was deepened because he had not acted on his personal wish to make Raphael a cardinal.

GIANTS ~ THE PEOPLE

Chigi's "Pleasure Palace" *(Rome)*

 Raphael's "Triumph of Galatea" is one of the epic paintings that was created for his friend Agostino Chigi's personal palace loggia.

Many of Raphael's friends treated him with abundant deference, due to his amorous nature with women that led him to quickly (and delightfully) service their whims on MANY occasions. Once in a while he would fall so completely in love with one of these women that it would truly interfere with the production of his work. So one day when his dear friend Agostino Chigi commissioned him to decorate a loggia in his palace in Rome, Raphael, because he was so distracted by his love of a particular woman, was not able to execute this task for his friend. So Chigi, knowing what to do in order to motivate his friend, learned of the identity of the woman who possessed the heart of Raphael, Margherita Luti (la Fornarina) and had her brought to his palace where he invited her to stay in a location that was near to where Raphael was painting. And it was in this way that the work became finished.
[Cherchez la femme - Look for the woman!]

The Earth Moved

Raphael was born on Good Friday in 1483 and died on his 37th birthday in 1520. On the day of his death, Pandolfo Pico della Mirandola wrote to the Duchess of Mantua. He attributed the cracks that appeared on this Good Friday in Raphael's Vatican Loggia to be a replay of the tremors that were felt when Christ died.

"Raphael and Friend"
a painting by Raphael

Epitaph on Raphael's Tomb: "By whom, while alive, Mother Nature feared defeat, and with whom, upon his death, she feared herself to die too."

Finding Raphael Today

With one of the largest and certainly the busiest workshops in Florence and Rome, Raphael was considered to be one of the most prolific artists in history and was able to produce a huge number of individual works that are now scattered around the world.

❀ Inside the Palatine Gallery at the **Pitti Palace**, you will see the stunning portraits of Agnolo Doni and Maddalena Doni and the portrait of Tommaso Inghirami. There are also displayed the La Donna Velata (the Woman with a Veil), the portrait of Cardinal Bibbiena, Ezechiel's Vision, the Madonna of the Grand Duke, characterized by the red dress and the light blue cloak, and the famous Madonna della Seggiola characterized by a gentle and unusual tenderness.

❀ In the **Uffizi Gallery** in The Correggio Room and in The Raphael and Andrea del Sarto Room are displayed the gorgeous Madonna of the Goldfinch, the portrait of Pope Leo X with Cardinals Giulio de' Medici & Luigi de' Rossi, the portraits of the Grand Dukes of Urbino, Elisabetta Gonzaga and Guidobaldo da Montefeltro. In addition, please admire the most famous of Raphael's self-portraits created in 1506 at 23 years of age.

Works created during his Florentine period 1504-1507: a portrait of Elisabetta Gonzaga, the portrait of Pietro Bembo, a self-portrait, Madonna of the Grand Duke, The Ansidei Madonna, Young Man with an Apple, Madonna Terranuova, The Madonna of the Goldfinch, Madonna del Prato, Orleans Madonna, La Donna Gravida, portrait of Maddalena Doni, Madonna of the Pinks, Young Woman with Unicorn, Madonna with Beardless St. Joseph, Saint Catherine of Alexandria, Canigiani Holy Family, La Belle Jardinière, The Deposition of Christ (The Entombment), The Three Theological Virtues, portrait of a Young Woman, The Holy Family with the Lamb, The Tempi Madonna, La Madonna de Bogotá

Raphael in the World

Because of the sheer number of works by Raphael, you will find a variety of collections scattered throughout the world. Outside of Italy, you will find more excellent works of Raphael in the National Gallery of Art in Washington DC and in the Getty Museum in Los Angeles, California - both in the US, in the Paris Louvre, the Sao Paolo Museum of Art in Brazil, the Gemäldegalerie in Berlin, the National Gallery in London, the Hermitage in St. Petersburg, the Metropolitan Museum of Art in New York City, the Alte Pinakothek in Munich, and scores more.

Nearly 300 years after his death (1833), Raphael's tomb was opened and his bones revealed him to be a mere 5' 2" (157cm), with beautiful teeth, a long neck, delicate arms and chest, with strong legs and feet. And because his large larynx was still intact, it was concluded that he had a deep and loud voice.

THE PEOPLE ~ GIANTS

BENVENUTO CELLINI

1500 - 1571

- One of the most important 'Mannerist' artists
- Tempestuous disposition
- Known mainly through his autobiography

GIANTS ~ THE PEOPLE

Cellini was a gifted artist of paint and of sculpture, a draftsman, a soldier and a musician. He was often commissioned to produce some fine items of gold, and some of stone. He was known for his unique skills in the craftsmanship of small items such as exquisite brooches that would both please and amuse the ladies with finery. In addition he decorated buttons of gold to be worn on the uniforms of military and political leaders.

He 'cut his teeth' by working in miniature, and became quite well-known for his peerless creations of rings, pendants and clasps for the ladies, and meticulously refined weapons for the men.

Bust of Benvenuto Cellini that sits on the Ponte Vecchio bridge

Although relatively few of his pieces remain today, they clearly reflect the genius of this temperamental Renaissance man. We know most about his life from his own autobiography. Cellini was one of the few Renaissance artists that took the time to create a journal (later to become his autobiography) of his life. In his writings, he was quite open about the many scrapes with the law and with many individuals throughout his life. For example, at age 19 he was arrested for fighting in public (not an unusual occurrence for him) and was sentenced to banishment from Florence. His temper was displayed easily and regularly, and from his own point of view, he simply did not understand why people wanted to get in his way so often. "Why is everyone so stupid?" He was not shy about raising a fist or with wielding a duel-challenging sword to ward off the many adversaries who simply did not understand him. Alas, poor Benvenuto.

Barroom Brawl

One evening while dining out with some of his artist friends, who spent the evening in uproarious joviality, he overheard a man in the room loudly proclaiming something to the effect of "Those rude people must be Florentines. But then again, aren't ALL Florentines rude?" Benvenuto approached the man and said "Are you the man who speaks so ill of Florentines?" And the man replied, "I am that man." Bunching his fist, Cellini swiftly delivered it into the face of that man and said, "Well sir, I am THIS man!" At this, both men drew their swords, ready for instant battle, but Cellini's friends quickly pulled him away while he shouted rebukes all the way back to their table.

Mannerist Art

Mannerism is a term which is widely contested among art circles. Generally speaking, it refers to Italian art that encompassed the late Renaissance era, and preceded the Baroque period. Subjects within a piece may have elongated or exaggerated limbs or torsos. This style can be found in some of Michelangelo's later works, Cellini's works, and in some Raphael pieces, among many others.

Goldsmith ◆ Painter ◆ Sculptor
Soldier ◆ Draftsman ◆ Musician ◆ Author

I Told You So!

Cosimo I de' Medici asked Cellini to create a bronze statue for him. Cellini pondered and chose to create the Greek god Perseus the moment after he beheaded the Gorgon Medusa. After carefully creating the full-sized wax figure, he went back to Medici for approval before he took the final step and cast the molten bronze.

Cosimo, formally educated in the fine arts, laughed and said "My dear friend, you cannot possibly make this statue. There are far too many pieces sticking out of it; there will be no way to get the hot bronze to fill all of those tiny areas."

Undaunted, Cellini pushed forth and began the bronzing process. But soon he saw that his friend Cosimo was correct, so he ordered his apprentices to add more wood to the fire to raise the temperature to melt the bronze thinner. And still it did not work. So he ordered his assistants to add anything they can find into the fire: large items like chairs, tables and ultimately large furniture. This worked, for the fire heated the bronze to a thin molten liquid that then flowed beautifully into all of the cracks and crevices of his Perseus.

Upon presenting it to Medici, he said, "See Cosimo, it was easy. I told you it would work!"

139

GIANTS ~ THE PEOPLE

LITTLE KNOWN SECRET: *At the Piazza dei Lanzi, climb up on the stage and walk around BEHIND Cellini's statue of Perseus. Look closely at the back of his head. You may have to move around so that the light cooperates with you, but you will see Cellini's own face!*

The front door of the Palazzo Vecchio is guarded on one side by Michelangelo's "David" and on the other side, by Bandinelli's "Hercules." They each symbolize the Republic: how the little guy can beat the big guy. From where "Perseus" is perched on the outdoor stage in the Loggia dei Lanzi, it may appear as though the head of the Gorgon Medusa is staring right at "David" turning him to stone. Translation: Since the "David" is a symbol of the success of the Republic, the Republic has now been turned into stone by Medusa ~ symbolically speaking, of course.

This salt box "Saliera" while displayed in Munich's Kunsthistorisches Museum, disappeared during a robbery of that museum in 2003. The piece was found three years later and returned to the same museum.

"The Firebrand of Florence" ...so stated Ira Gershwin and Kurt Weill

Cellini was, self-admittedly, a hot head. In his autobiography, he had wondered throughout most of his life, why everyone else was so rude, and why everywhere he went, people angered him. Because of this, he has become known since then as "The Firebrand of Florence." And because of his torrid disposition, he has been mentioned quite often in literature, poetry and song.

Cellini's life is an occasional point of reference in the writings of Mark Twain. Cellini's autobiography is one of the books Tom Sawyer mentions as inspiration while freeing Jim in the ***Adventures of Huckleberry Finn.***

His work is mentioned in ***The Prince and the Pauper*** in Chapter VII: "Its furniture was all of massy gold, and beautified with designs which well-nigh made it priceless, since they were the work of Benvenuto." In ***A Connecticut Yankee in King Arthur's Court*** chapter XVII, Cellini is alluded to as the "epitome of brutal, immoral, and yet deeply religious aristocracy."

Herman Melville compares his character Ahab, at the captain's first appearance, to a sculpture by Cellini. From ***Moby Dick***; "His whole high, broad form, seemed made of solid bronze, and shaped in an unalterable mould, like Cellini's cast of Perseus."

The fictional secret agent, Nick Carter, owns a pearl-handled 400-year-old stiletto said to have been made by Cellini, which is featured regularly in the 260+ novels in the series.

ACADÉMIE ROYALE DE MUSIQUE.

AUJOURD'HUI LUNDI 10 SEPTEMBRE 1838,

La PREMIÈRE Représentation de

BENVENUTO

CELLINI,

OPÉRA en DEUX actes.

Upon reading Cellini's autobiography, Hector Berlioz was so struck with Cellini's lifelong dramatic episodes that he was inspired to create an opera around Cellini's tumultuous life. This is the poster that was created to promote its first performance in 1838.

Hide Me ~ PLEASE!

After yet another fray that, according to his autobiography, included attempted murder of a 'deserving' man, Cellini was chased by eight of the man's shovel-and-pitchfork-wielding clan members.

In escape, Cellini ran toward the Church of Santa Maria Novella where he saw Fra Alessio Strozzi, whereupon he pleaded "For the love of God dear Father, please save my life!"

Agreeing, the monk hid Cellini in a tiny room behind the church. Soon the gang approached the church shouting that no matter where he hid, he would be found, and anyone who harbored him would suffer dearly. The good father kept silent until the boys moved on. When all seemed quiet, the monk appeared with an armful of women's clothes and told Cellini to put them on and to run like the wind. And thus, Cellini managed to escape yet another self-initiated confrontation.

THE PEOPLE ~ GIANTS

GIANTS ~ THE PEOPLE

GIORGIO VASARI
1511-1574

- Built the mysterious passageway "The Vasari Corridor"
- "Spin Doctor" for the Grand Duke Cosimo I de' Medici
- Coined the term "Renaissance"
- Designed the Uffizi
- Renovated Santa Croce, Santa Maria Novella
- Author of "Lives of the Artists"

Although he is a known entity among schooled artists, Giorgio Vasari's name has not been passed down often enough through history to reach today's mainstream classrooms. However, the recent novel "Inferno" by Dan Brown (Doubleday) has given a whole new mystique to Vasari largely because of the significant role played by the mysterious Vasari Corridor in that book. Ticket sales for visits to the Vasari Corridor have sky-rocketed since that publication in 2013.

Vasari was born in the Tuscan town of Arezzo, and was trained early in life as a painter and a sculptor in the schools of Michelangelo and Raphael, among others. As an 'independent contractor,' he created a large and successful workshop which produced paintings for many notable entities such as the Catholic Church and the **Medici family**. He traveled to Rome and the countryside creating frescoes and decorating ceilings

Giorgio Vasari: a Self Portrait

for a long list of patrons. His best-known works, however, still reside in Florence. Some of his more enduring works can be seen in places such as the ceiling and walls in the "Salon di Cinquecento" (Hall of 500) inside the **Palazzo Vecchio**, on the ceiling of the **Uffizi Gallery**, and the inside of the beautiful cupola at the **Basilica of Santa Maria del Fiore, or "Il Duomo."**

As an architect, he is known chiefly for his design of the **Vasari Corridor. This over-ground tunnel is still today considered to be** an architectural marvel that spans nearly a full kilometer over the city. He was also the designer of one of the most visited museums in the world today,

Architect ◆ *Painter* ◆ *Marketing/PR*
Engineer ◆ *Writer* ◆ *Art Historian*

In Dan Brown's run-away best-selling novel "Inferno" (Doubleday), the main characters, in an effort to flee unseen from the bad guys, found the secret entrance to the mysterious Vasari Corridor and warily traversed it. Were they successful? Perhaps. Gotta read the book. ;-)

the **Uffizi Gallery**. Additionally, he was responsible for the renovation of both Cathedrals of **Santa Croce** and **Santa Maria Novella**.

A close friend and ally of **Cosimo I de' Med**ici, Vasari, being a member of the 'cognoscenti' (an 'insider'), was privy to a whole keg of the Duke's royal secrets. Because of his gift with words, he acted as a kind of P.R. guy for Medici. Some feel that in his writings (some of which can neither be proven nor disproven), he made sure that his friend and chief patron Cosimo I was universally depicted in a more-than-warranted positive light, and has been nicknamed by some as "The Spin Doctor for the Medici."

Back in his hometown of Arezzo, Vasari created a fine home for himself and his family, which has been converted into a museum known as Museo Casa Vasari. Due to his popularity and his considerable influence he was elected gonfaloniere for Florence, a position somewhat similar to a 'mayor'.

Giorgio Vasari died in Florence in 1574, and was buried in Arezzo. ✿

One of the more famous works by Vasari is in the cupola of the Duomo. "The Last Judgment" was a project that was shared by Federico Zuccari. After Vasari's death, Zuccari finished the work incorporating many 'suggestions' from a variety of other artists. The trained eye, however, may be able to point out the inconsistencies that resulted from that array of input.

143

The term "Renaissance" (French for 'Rebirth') was first coined by Giorgio Vasari to describe the specific era of Free Thinking (or awakening) that occurred in Western Europe roughly between 1320 and 1550, that was voiced through an explosion of art, architecture, and science.

This magnificent room within the Palazzo Vecchio, the Studiolo of Francesco I (Grand Duke of Tuscany) was designed in all her magnificence by Giorgio Vasari.

"Salone dei Cinquecento" (Room of 500) in Palazzo Vecchio is covered with Vasari paintings, some of which have replaced great frescoes by da Vinci and Michelangelo.

The First Art Historian

Giorgio Vasari fancied himself to be quite an art maven. He was after all an artist schooled by Michelangelo and Raphael, as well as an architect by education. Because of his lifelong friendship with Cosimo I de' Medici, Vasari was on the inside track as he hob-nobbed with many of the famous artists of the mid-to-late Renaissance period.

Adding one more talent to his impressively-growing list of abilities, he wrote about his own observances of and his experiences with his fellow artists and architects. Originally titled Lives of the Most Excellent Painters, Sculptors,

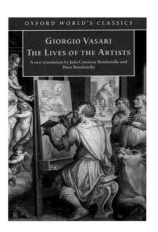

and Architects he poured out his knowledge of the most famous artists that influenced the Renaissance era.

Vasari was one of a mere handful of writers who was personally active in the burgeoning art movement at that time, hence much of what was stated in his book has been characterized as historical truth. However, some critics feel that he was the "public relations" expert for the Medici, and that his perspectives might be 'skewed' and he may have described the Medici in a brighter light than was the actual truth.

Nevertheless, his influence during this famous period is unmistakable, as was his long-standing paid relationship with the Medici. Vasari's book is considered to be the first art history book in European history. But because of the mere smattering of information available to corroborate some of his facts, it is not entirely known which details in his book (if any) have been exaggerated or manufactured.

David's Broken Arm

During a riotous Florentine upheaval in 1527, a bunch of local citizens fled to the top of the Palazzo Vecchio, where in an effort to thwart their attackers, they threw things down through the crenellated rooftop. Large things. Scary things. Things that really hurt. One of those things, something large and heavy like a rugged dining room table (and probably the chairs too!) crashed down upon Michelangelo's beautiful sculpture of David, who

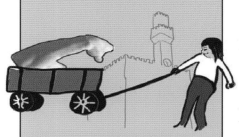

stood innocently in the piazza below, and broke his arm into three pieces.

Along came a boy pulling a wagon. When he saw the pieces of the broken statue, he picked up the rather large pieces of the statue, put them into his wagon and lugged them home.

Many years later as an adult, he produced those broken pieces to aid in the repair of the City's beloved David.

That little boy, according to legend, was Giorgio Vasari.

GIANTS ~ THE PEOPLE

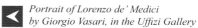
*Portrait of Lorenzo de' Medici
by Giorgio Vasari, in the Uffizi Gallery*

"Mutilation of Uranus" by Giorgio Vasari can be found inside the Palazzo Vecchio.

Vestiges of Vasari are quite easy to find throughout the city of Florence and the surrounding Tuscan towns, as so much of his work has remained splendidly intact. They are some of the most visible of those works left behind by the Renaissance Giants. He has touched nearly every important building or structure that you see today.

Finding Vasari Today

🌸 Vasari's most notable paintings are the beautiful frescoes in the Salone dei Cinquecento in the Palazzo Vecchio. They depict the battle victories of Florence over Pisa, Siena, Porto Ercole and Leghorn (Livorno). These gigantic works of art are said to be covering the original war paintings created by da Vinci and Michelangelo. But this has yet to be proven.

🌸 The inside of the Duomo is a work of art in and of itself. Vasari's fresco, which can be seen in the cupola of the Duomo is simply frosting on the cake.

Loggia del Vasari in Arezzo, Italy.

Finding Vasari Today

🌸 Vasari was hired by Cosimo I de' Medici to remodel the Palazzo Vecchio itself.

🌸 The Uffizi Gallery was designed by Vasari as the new offices of the city officials. Today, nearly 1.5 million people cross its threshold.

🌸 Vasari designed the remodel of the Pitti Palace for Cosimo I de' Medici and his wife Eleanor of Toledo.

🌸 Other Vasari-designed or remodelled Structures include:
The Basilica of Santa Maria Novella, Boboli Gardens, Villa Giulia, Palazzo della Carovana (in Pisa), and Santa Croce.

GALILEO GALILEI
THE SKY IS NOT THE LIMIT
1564-1642

- Taught mathematics and music
- Developed: important Laws of Physics
- Invented important technology
- Discovered: Jupiter's moons, super nova, Saturn,
- planetary orbital paths and sun spots
- Tried by the Inquisition for heresy
- Lost his sight completely

With a healthy preoccupation with everything related to both space as well as time, Galileo felt that if a person could master those two subjects, they could unravel the secrets of the universe. For example, they could determine longitude, reckon whether the Earth actually moved and at what speed, calculate the distance of faraway planets and stars, and apply the principles of balance. This knowledge helped to improve the telescope, and create a compass that would enable an explorer to circumnavigate the Earth predictably. He invented the thermoscope (the first thermometer), the pendulum clock, and made it possible to create the first microscope. In addition, Galileo's genius helped to improve military devices and weaponry.

Because of his free-wheeling curiosity and indefatigable genius, the man behind this inconceivable mind represents the end of the Renaissance period. Our Gallery of Giants would not be complete without him.

People commonly believe that Galileo invented the telescope. On the contrary, he merely improved the lens technology that made it possible to see further away and more clearly. Unfortunately, his experiments while looking directly into the sun tragically caused a complete and permanent blindness in him.
His improvements over the 'lens' also went the other way: they helped to create and improve the microscope as well.

Galileo formulated the theories that made it possible for others to inven
scientific tools, devices and technology in general.

*The measuring rule (below), made by
Hans Christoph Schissler, was used for
military purposes. This included the ability
to determine the calibers of stone and lead
projectiles, land surveys, and to reckon time.
Accordingly, there is a scale of weights for
cannonballs, a linear measurement scale in
Roman feet, a small magnetic compass in
the leg joint, a viewer at the end of one leg,
and a cross-arm with the scale of diurnal
hours. A second cross-arm and plumb bob
(missing) enabled the instrument to be used
as a gunner's level for measuring inclina-
tions and adjusting gun elevation.*

~Museo Galileo

*This item exemplifies the
celebration of Galileo
as a hero and martyr of
science. The finger was
detached from his body
nearly 100 years after his
death. It was eventually
moved to the Museo di
Storia della Scienza in
1927. On the marble
base is carved a com-
memorative inscription
by Tommaso Perelli.*
~ Museo Galileo

GIANTS ~ THE PEOPLE

THE TRAGIC END OF A BEAUTIFUL MIND

Born in Pisa to a well-known music theorist and accomplished lutenist, Galileo, like his father, easily adopted the lute and became quite proficient with it.

Galileo was a firm believer in heliocentrism, an understanding that all of the planets revolved around the Sun - instead of the accepted belief that the whole universe revolved around the Earth. His many scientific beliefs were considered to be far-fetched ideas, and so brought him under the scrutiny of the dreaded Tribunal. Although the Church had largely 'gone along' with his 'scientific rants,' they soon changed their attitude when he published his book Dialogue Concerning the Two Chief World Systems, which was considered to be confrontational to the Pope and contrary to the Church Doctrine.

He was tried by the Tribunal of the Roman Inquisition and was required to confess his sins and recant his scientific teachings. Under the threat of torture, he recanted and so was sentenced to house arrest for the remainder of his life. In addition, his books were placed on the List of Forbidden (banned) Books. The Church had at last managed to silence Galileo.

While living out his exile in Florence, the lawyers of the seriously ill Galileo petitioned the courts to allow Galileo to return to Rome to seek medical assistance.

These requests were refused.

Galileo facing the Roman Inquisition.

Blind, sick and grieving for the death of his beloved daughter Sister Maria Celeste, he died a sad and lonely death in his home in Florence.

The city of Florence has always regretted the bad treatment of Galileo and has since made sincere efforts to keep his memory alive.

THE LIFE

1464	1574	1579	1581	1583	1585	1586	1587	1589	1592	1595
Galileo was Born	Family moved to Florence	Wanted to join a Monastery	Graduated from University of Arts	Studied Math & Physics	Returned to Florence without degree	Chose Archimedes over Aristotle	Invented Hydrostatic Balance / Taught Math in Florence / Surpassed Archimedes on principles of the Center of Gravity	Taught Math in Pisa	Dropped weights from Leaning Tower / Father died	Chaired Math Dept @U / Invented Water / Defi

FLORENCE   ROME   PISA   PADUA

Physicist ✦ Mathematician ✦ Philosopher
Astrophysicist ✦ Artist ✦ Musician

Galileo 'performed' often at the behest of his most favored patrons: The (Medici) Grand Dukes of Tuscany. He was considered to be quite a crowd pleaser, and some even felt that he was performing magic tricks, rather than feats of science.

OF GALILEO

...ship w/Marina Gamba
Marina had Daughter: (Virginia) Maria Celeste
Borrowed money for Sister's Dowry
Marina has 2nd Daughter: (Livia) Sister Arcangela
Developed Pendulum Theory
Developed Law of Falling Bodies
Discovered Supernova
Invented 1st Thermometer
Developed Hydrostatics
Refined Accelerated Motion
Made a Telescope
Astronomical Observations
Discovered Jupiter's Moons
Kepler supported Galileo

1600 1602 1604 1606 1608 1610

Playing for Protection

Cosimo I de' Medici, **the Grand Duke of Tuscany,** not having received a religious education during his upbringing, possessed a natural bent for the sciences. During his reign (1609 - 1621) as Grand Duke he enjoyed, like his Medici predecessors, patronizing the arts & sciences. When Cosimo I was a child, Galileo was one of his favorite teachers and they enjoyed a life-long friendship.

Galileo served two main functions during Cosimo I's rule: that of a teacher to the current batch of Medici children, and also as an 'entertainer' within the courts where he would amaze, amuse, and delight audiences with his masterful scientific demonstrations, 'tricks' and explanations. As long as he made himself available for these two functions, he enjoyed the lavish financial support needed to pursue his scientific research, and the prestigious protection of the Grand Duke of Tuscany.

Late Renaissance Swing

One day during a visit to a Cathedral, Galileo noticed that the breeze was blowing high in the church causing the chandeliers to gently sway. He timed the swings with the beating of his heart. This led him, after further study, to notice that each swing of the chandelier took the same amount of time to swing - regardless of the distance of the swing. This, in turn, led him to further ponder the principles of the pendulum, about which he concluded that only the length of the pendulum itself would affect the time of a swing, not the distance it had to travel. In addition, he recognized that a pendulum swings the fastest at the bottom of the arc - it did not travel at the same speed throughout the entire arc as previously expected.

NOTE: Although Galileo lived AFTER the **High** Renaissance period, he too was supported by the Medici. The influence of the Renaissance contributed significantly to the free-minded scientific pursuits as well as his personal perspectives and attitudes, which have in turn earned him an important and everlasting position in scientific, Florentine, and global history.

THE PEOPLE ~ GIANTS

CE • FATHER OF OBSERVATIONAL ASTRONOMY • FATHER OF MODERN PHYSICS • FATHER OF MODERN SCIENCE • FATHER OF SCIENCE

Galileo the Artist?

Galileo was accomplished in the musical and the visual arts. Like his father, he was a known lutenist. In addition to teaching the highest levels of mathematics, he taught the advanced art concepts of perspective and chiaroscuro at the Florence Academy of Art & Design.

GALILEO GALILEI

Galileo travelled to Pisa and decided that the Leaning Tower was a perfect place to test his theory about the rate of descent of different sized, shaped and weighted objects. Which items will fall faster?

Finding Galileo Today

The best place to find Galileo in Florence is within the exemplary Museo Galileo next to the Uffizi Gallery. Plan extra time: the exhibits are excellent and the children's area is quite enjoyable.

...ather
...s Kepler died
Attempted to clear Censorship
Plague struck Florence
Begin Florence Inquisition
Pope Urban VIII sided with Inquisitors
Too sick to appear in Rome, then
Forced to appear in Rome
Trial & Imprisonment
Threatened, then Recanted
House arrest in Sienna, then Florence
Continued to Publish
Suffered hernia
Requested medical treatment in Rome
Medical requests denied
Maria Celeste died
Lost total eyesight
Medical requests denied
Galileo Died.

1632   1633   1634   1638   1642

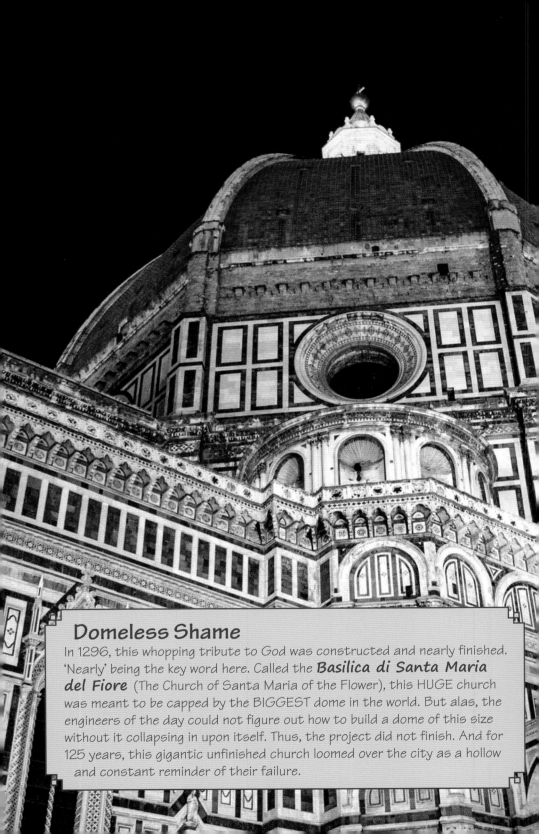

Domeless Shame

In 1296, this whopping tribute to God was constructed and nearly finished. 'Nearly' being the key word here. Called the **Basilica di Santa Maria del Fiore** (The Church of Santa Maria of the Flower), this HUGE church was meant to be capped by the BIGGEST dome in the world. But alas, the engineers of the day could not figure out how to build a dome of this size without it collapsing in upon itself. Thus, the project did not finish. And for 125 years, this gigantic unfinished church loomed over the city as a hollow and constant reminder of their failure.

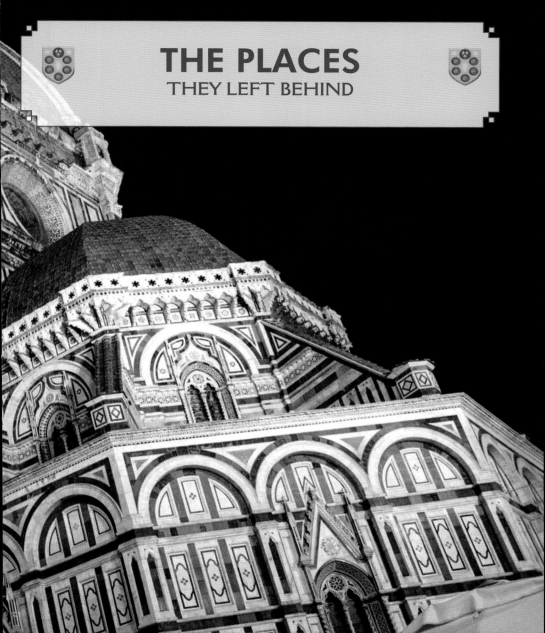

THE PLACES
THEY LEFT BEHIND

The Gates to Paradise

On the east side of the Baptistery you will find an astonishing piece of art: the **Baptistery doors.** These bronze beauties were created by **Lorenzo Ghiberti** who took 25 years to make them. Each panel tells a story (20 scenes in all) from the life of John the Baptist. **Michelangelo,** after laying eyes upon this incredible art in bronze, adequately nick-named the doors "The Gates to Paradise."

TWO CROWDED PIAZZAS

The Baptistery, the Campanile, the Church and the Duomo are snuggled together in Piazza del Duomo and Piazza di Giovanni as a proud and massive tribute to God. The Duomo has become the main symbol of the city of Florence today.

8-sided Battistero di San Giovanni
(The Baptistery)

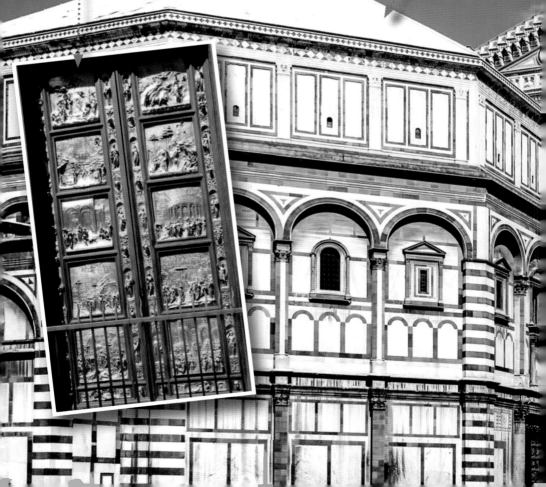

*The Duomo & the Campanile
dominate the night.*

The Campanile, *aka
Giotto's Bell Tower*

*Cathedral of **Santa
Maria del Fiore***

il Duomo

*The statue of Filippo Brunelleschi sits
proudly against a wall in the Piazza del
Duomo admiring the fruits of his labor
for all of eternity.*

IL DUOMO
HOW TO TURN SHAME INTO VICTORY
Located in the Piazza del Duomo

Construction of il Duomo was started in 1296. Originally meant to exhibit the massive extent of their devoutness, it was going to be the largest dome in the world. Her engineers, however, soon discovered a flagon full of problems in the design of such a massive dome. The most daunting issue was how to keep the structure from collapsing inward as they built it up during construction. Time and time again, this same problem reared its ugly head as teams of builders were called upon to figure out how to create the dome without it collapsing during the process. But to no avail for many years to come. And so the cathedral remained as a reminder of failure and shame for the local Florentines for **135 years!**

Somewhere around 1420, a shy gold smith who also happened to be a self-taught engineer named **Filippo Brunelleschi**, was seen wandering the streets of Florence. In his head he tried to solve the myriad of construction issues that had plagued the completion of the Duomo. He drew sketches then tossed them aside; he talked to himself endlessly as he attempted solutions. He went days without food and sleep as he pondered the puzzle that he knew would some day become a dome.

After losing a competition to design the great bronze doors of the **Baptistery** next to the Duomo (*p74*), Brunelleschi and his buddy **Donatello** took a trip to Rome. There he learned important engineering techniques from ancient Roman structures, such as the Pantheon, ones that he felt may help him to solve the overwhelming construction issues back home. Upon his return to Florence, he went to some of the most influential folks in town, excitedly raving about his ideas and solutions.

Meanwhile, Giovanni de' Medici, a wealthy banker, upstart politician, and new-comer to the Florentine social scene, was looking for a special project that would propel his political influence into the stratosphere ~ and he found one. By providing the money and the support required to complete the construction of the monstrous embarrassment that loomed over his beloved city, he would be able to amass enough power and influence to propel himself into a stronger role of leadership. Enter his soon-to-be best friend, Filippo Brunelleschi *p68*.

Notice the sheer immensity of the Duomo as compared to the size of the people at the bottom of this photo. The massiveness of the <u>Church of Santa Maria del Fiore</u> with her monstrous dome dominates the Florentine skyline. For nearly 450 years (1436–1881) she held the record as the largest brick and mortar dome in the world. Today, schools of architecture keep il Duomo as a strong part of their curriculum; its technical marvels have held architects and engineers in awe for over 600 years.

GEMS ~ PLACES

David was originally supposed to be put in a little niche high up in the church. Had this happened, he would have disappeared into religious obscurity and the world would not have had their beloved David to admire for all time to come.

Look up: The inside of the dome boasts a detailed & scenic fresco of "The Last Judgment" started by Giorgio Vasari, and because of his death, was later completed by one of his students, Federico Zuccari.

When you ascend the 463 steps that lead up into the Dome, notice that you will be climbing between the two layers (far-left) of this massive structure. The double-layered technique is one of the secrets to the strength that was built into the dome created by Filippo Brunelleschi's extensive genius. Reaching the top will give you the added treat of looking out over the city from the cupola.

MUSEO dell'OPERA del DUOMO
Located in the Piazza del Duomo

1.

Located next to il Duomo is the Museo dell'Opera del Duomo, who's grand reconstruction was completed in 2015. Dedicated specifically to the history and the construction of the Dome, it exhibits over 200 extremely important and rare treasures.

- Implements used by Brunelleschi during construction of the Dome, such as pulleys, trolleys and brick molds.

- Lorenzo Ghiberti's original "Gate to Paradise" (1) can be found here, as only a replica can be found today on the outside of the Baptistery.

- Michelangelo's poignant "Deposition" aka "Florence Pieta" (2) can be admired from all sides.

- Two choir lofts that historically existed under the Dome are now protected in this museum. One was created by the famous Donatello and the other by Luca della Robbia.

- Donatello's original penitent "Mary Magdalen" (3) A copy stands outside of the Palazzo del Vecchio.

- Stroll outside onto the Terrazza del Brunelleschi and treat yourself to a breath-taking view of his spectacular and unmatched Duomo.

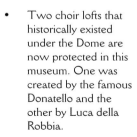

2.

3.

PLACES ~ GEMS

GEMS ~ PLACES

SANTA MARIA del FIORE
CHURCH of SANTA MARIA of the FLOWERS
Located in the Piazza del Duomo

The vertical impact that is felt as you stand beneath the lofty Gothic ceiling was intentional from its original design. Note the tiny size of the tour group in the lower right side of this photo.

*Residing on the west wall you will find Domenico di Micheli-no's famous painting of Dante holding his poem **The Divine Comedy**. Within this painting is a rendering of the levels of hell, purgatory and paradise (with Adam and Eve), along with the celestial spheres. Embedded is Florence, the city responsible for both joy and poignant sadness for Dante himself.*

UCCELLO'S MOST UNUSUAL CLOCK

Over the door you will find a very interesting item: The Clock. Designed by Paolo Uccello, there are several things to notice:

- The numbers begin at the bottom of the clock instead of the top. It is a 24-hour clock, and the '1' and the '24' are on the bottom.

- The numbers, ergo the hands, move in a counter clockwise direction. It wasn't until the 1600's that Europe standardized the clock direction as the opposite of this. Uccello created the clock this way because this was how sun dials worked, and this was how people were used to seeing a 'clock.'

- Galileo created a pendulum for this clock.

- The Four Evangelists are depicted in the corners

- The striking Shooting Star hands were also designed by Uccello.

BAPTISTERY
BATTISTERO DI SAN GIOVANNI
Located in the Piazza del Duomo

Huddled shyly in the shadow of the looming but impressive Duomo sits the Baptistery of San Giovanni. Rebuilt and consecrated during the 11th century as a Christian Baptistery, records show that an octagonal religious building stood in this spot since around the 6th century. This eight-sided structure is an excellent example of Romanesque architecture. This was one of the ancient structures that influenced Brunelleschi and until today, scores of other architects as well. In fact, the Baptistery, the Basilica, and the Duomo are staples in most schools of architecture around the world today.

A view from the Southwest creates the false impression that the Baptistery dominates this massive foursome in the Piazza del Duomo.

For approximately 800 years (until the late 1800's) all Catholic citizens born in Florence were baptized here. Some of the most notable names are Cosimo I de' Medici - the Grand Duke of Tuscany, Dante Alighieri, Carlo (Collodi) Lorenzini (the author of Pinnocchio), the Antipope John XXIII (Pirate Pope) *p34*, among scores of others.

Of the three doors, the oldest is on the South side of the Baptistery. Andrea Pisano created them in the mid-1330's. In the 2 upper panels are conveyed the scenes from the life of John the Baptist, while the others depict Christian virtues.

North
2nd Doors were designed by Ghiberti 1401 - 1424

East
3rd Doors designed by Ghiberti "Gates to Paradise" 1425 - 1452

South
1st Doors were created by Pisano – 1330
Life of John the Baptist

The Northern door tells the stories of the New Testament in the 20 upper panels, and the 4 Evangelists and 4 Church Fathers in the remaining.

The East door is the most sublime of them all. Called the "Gate to Paradise" by Michelangelo, it was the object of the heated art competition *p74* between Lorenzo Ghiberti and Filippo Brunelleschi. Ghiberti ultimately won the competition, taking an astounding 25 years to complete this rather sumptuous work of art.

The Baptistery's Octagonal Ceiling

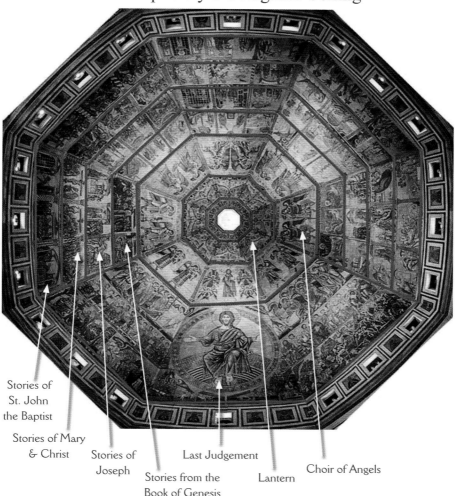

Stories of
St. John
the Baptist

Stories of Mary
& Christ

Stories of
Joseph

Last Judgement

Stories from the
Book of Genesis

Lantern

Choir of Angels

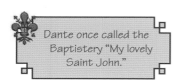

Dante once called the
Baptistery "My lovely
Saint John."

Inside the Baptistery, you will find the tomb of the Baldesarre Cossa -
Antipope John the XXIII. Cosimo (the elder) de' Medici hired Donatello
and Michelozzo to create the tomb. Note the unique canopy over a sleeping An-
tipope. Also notice that he is not facing up toward heaven, rather, he is looking
out over the room. Was this because he was defrocked as as Pope?

GATES OF PARADISE

This was **Ghiberti's** *second commission to create doors for the* **Baptistery.** *His first project as a contest winner was to create 20 panels from the New Testament which filled a different entryway.*

Lorenzo Ghiberti believed in putting himself into his work.  *He is peeking out for all eternity in a pleased and silent watch as the passersby enjoy his lavish doors. The figure just to the right of his image is that of his son Vittorio who worked by his side in the Ghiberti workshop.*

"Condussi detta opera con grandissima diligentia e con grandissimo amore."

"I made this work with the greatest diligence and the greatest love."
~ *Lorenzo Ghiberti*

PLACES ~ GEMS

In the early 1400's, a contest (*p74*) was set up to attract an artist/architect to design the east doors of the Baptistery (pg. 74).

Ghiberti used the "lost wax" method (*p97*) to cast the bronze reliefs on the panels of the east doors. Each panel depicts a scene from the Old Testament. (Note: some panels illustrate a combination of multiple scenes.)

Lorenzo set to work to create this tribute to the Old Testament, and periodically his patrons would stop by to ask if the doors were finished yet. The answer was always a resounding 'Not yet'. This went on for nearly 25 years when finally Ghiberti announced that the doors were finished.

Ghiberti used a technique in which some of the 3D figures virtually jump out of the scene with such depth as to lend an air of plausible realism. This had never before been seen in Bronze works, and some have commented that "...Ghiberti 'painted' each scene with bronze."

This Baptistery is where all Catholic Florentines had been baptized including Dante Alighieri and the Medici.

CAMPANILE
GIOTTO'S BELL TOWER
Began in 1334

GEMS ~ PLACES

View from the Top
*Climbing 400+ steps to the top of the Campanile is a feat at any age. On the way up, you'll be treated to a variety of views at different heights of the famous **Duomo** next door. Approximately 3/4 of the way up, you'll get a resting break at the bell, and you will have the comfort of knowing that you'll soon be at the top to partake of the expansive views offered all around the tower. If you manage to time it at the end of a clear day, a sunset climb will reward you with one of the best souvenirs you could want: a sublime vista of this ancient city as the day slips into darkness!*

PLACES ~ GEMS

In 1334, Giotto designed the majestic Bell Tower to live next to the famous Baptistery of San Giovanni. He designed it to be 100 arms lengths at its base (25 each side) and 140 arms lengths high (84.7 meters; 277.8 feet). To crown the top of the tower, Giotto designed a four-sided pyramid. Keeping in mind that this tower was created using a traditional German architectural style, his fellow designers talked him out of the pyramid saying that the tower was perfect just the way it was.

In addition to designing the original model for the Bell Tower, Giotto also designed the marble scenes in relief for it.

The city of Florence was so excited that they celebrated this upcoming new addition to their skyline and proudly gave Giotto his Citizenship to Florence. In addition he was paid 100 gold florins per year - a vast and terrific fortune at that time.

Giotto never saw the completion of his campanile. After his death in 1337, the construction was continued by Andrea Pisano who faithfully followed Giotto's designs. It was finally completed in 1359 by Francesco Talenti.

THE UFFIZI GALLERY
HOME OF HISTORY'S MOST FAMOUS ART

The Uffizi (the Italian word for "Office") was designed by Giorgio Vasari in the mid-1500's at the wishes of Cosimo I de' Medici, the Grand Duke of Tuscany. He felt that the previous city offices in the Palazzo Vecchio were becoming a bit cramped because unlike his predecessors who ruled the city of Florence, he had a larger realm to command: all of Tuscany. And due to his recent conquests, Tuscany was growing in both size and complexity. Hence, a larger place to do business was needed.

It was built on the banks of the Arno River providing magnificent water views to its inhabitants. The U-shaped building creates the perfect space for public events to be hosted, such as political speeches and general public announcements. The building boasts spacious opulence while reflecting the simplistic symmetry that is considered to be of typical Renaissance architecture.

Today, the Uffizi is a gallery where over a million-and-a-half visitors come each year to feast their eyes on the incredible works of some of the greatest artists in all of western history. 🌸

The U-shaped building provides a shady spot that surrounds a piazza for local contemporary artists to show and sell their art today.

*The massive internal corridors are lined with sculptures and art-works arranged chrono-logically. The ceilings are covered in beautiful fres-coes painted by **Giorgio Vasari**. Fittingly, as he was also the architect of the building itself.*

The Uffizi snuggles up against the Arno River providing a tranquil reflection for her admirers in the local shops and res-taurants across the water.

GEMS ~ PLACES

GALLERIA dell' ACCADEMIA
WHERE DAVID LIVES

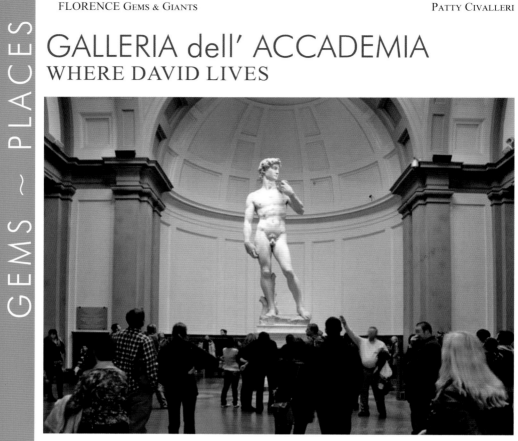

▲ *David was created by Michelangelo as a symbol of The Republic. It is an ideal example of how the virtues of goodness and perseverance can overcome (if indeed God is on your side) a much larger and looming evil (represented in this case by the unseen - and soon to be defeated - Goliath). Not only is 'David' the most popular sculpture in Florence, 'he' is considered to be the most photographed and duplicated sculpture in all the world.*

Bearded Slave   *Atlas Slave*   *Young Slave*   *Awakening Slave*

Accademia e Compagnia delle Arti del Disegno (The Academy and Company of Fine Arts & Design) was founded in 1563 by Cosimo I de' Medici, the Grand Duke of Tuscany. He compensated Giorgio Vasari for the architectural design. Medici's idea was to create an official place where masters could formally school all artists in all media.

The Academy was broken down into two parts: one part was set aside as a guild for all of the local working artisans. The other part was for the teaching academy itself, where artists would learn from the masters to perfect their individual styles. In the mid-1700s, the Accademia Gallery *(left)* was founded in an adjacent building to exhibit the finest works from the school.

Hall of Colossus ▶

The Renaissance *artist Giambologna accomplished new techniques when he created this emotional sculpture of "The Rape of the Sabine Women." It was the first sculpture where multiple figures were all carved from a single piece of stone. In addition, you will notice that unlike earlier sculptures of that time, there is no 'front' to this piece. It was created to be enjoyed from all perspectives equally. This is a plaster model; the original can be seen in Florence's open-air museum, the* Loggia dei Lanzi *(p233).*

MICHELANGELO'S "SLAVES"

◀ *As you approach Michelangelo's triumphant and beloved "David" at the end of the hall, take the time to enjoy his four "Prisoners'"(aka "Slaves") sculptures along the side walls. Originally intended for the tomb of Pope Julius II, they soulfully depict the excruciating process of 'escape' from the stone. It is arguable whether or not these are unfinished works, or whether Michelangelo's original intention was to depict a struggle in progress for freedom. Some argue that these may not be the actual work of Michelangelo at all, even though the rough chisel marks that are seen on these pieces are common in many of his later works. Judge for yourself.*

Michelangelo is known to have said that he never 'created' anything. But by simply removing the excess stone, he merely freed the figure that was already trapped within. Perhaps this is why his method of sculpting differs from others: where some would carve out the major shapes of a piece before chiselling the details, Michelangelo would start with a single area and soon that whole area would be nearly complete before he started on the next area. It almost seems as though he had the whole piece worked out in his head from the first moment he laid eyes on the stone.

PALAZZO VECCHIO
THE OLD PALACE

One of the most prominent sites on the Florentine skyline is the tall slender crenelated tower of the Palazzo Vecchio. Built initially to house the local government offices, it was designed with the majesty so deserving of an important city like Florence. Over the centuries, Palazzo Vecchio's name changed to reflect the rulers who took up office here over time.

The crenellated clock tower stands over the cube-shaped palace as if on perpetual guard for its citizens. It looks over the Piazza della Signoria and the Loggia dei Lanzi. Outside of the front doors, a 17-foot copy of Michelangelo's "David" stands in defiance as he stares down an unseen Goliath, ready to pitch his stone of death. Next to David stands the victorious Hercules poised over the defeated Cacus, a stunningly dramatic sculpture created by Baccio Bandinelli.

After the death of Lorenzo (il Magnifico) de' Medici in 1492, Girolamo Savonarola took over the Palazzo. After renovating to suit his own flair, he ruled the city using his threats of damnation to whip the citizens into conformity. After his eventual hanging in

Crenellations are the zigzag battlements that provide protection for soldiers and guards.

"Salone dei Cinquecento" (The Hall of 500) was built by Girolamo Savonarola after he took over from the failed Medici, to have a place where his Grand Council (Consiglio Maggiore) consisting of 500 members could meet. Later, when the Medici returned to power, Cosimo I hired Giorgio Vasari to enlarge this chamber so that his own court could preside here.

front of the building in 1497, several rulers took up residence here, including Cosimo I de' Medici, the Grand Duke of Tuscany over 50 years later. It is from here that you can peer out a window to see a marble tribute to him on horseback.

Today the two floors of the palace remain as a museum of Cosimo I and his family. You can tour through the large Salone dei Cinquecento (Hall of 500) where many city council meetings were held (below). Because Cosimo I now lived across the river but still worked here in the Palazzo Vecchio, he ordered his favorite architect Giorgio Vasari to create for him a private kilometer-long over-ground corridor that would lead safely from his home across the river to the Palazzo Vecchio, the office of Cosimo I.

GIANTS
Back-to-Back

It was difficult to decide which 'Giant' should decorate these hallowed halls with wall-sized visual stories to depict one of Florence's successful battles. So they decided to hire the two biggest names in the art world at that time: Leonardo da Vinci and Michelangelo. Da Vinci chose the Battle of Anghiari, and Michelangelo selected The Battle of Cascina. *(Can you imagine the verbal poison that flew around that room during this event?)* Over the years however, both of these paintings were lost, but some insist that clues exist in the current paintings, created by Giorgio Vasari, that give hints as to the current locations of these masterpieces of the past.
But do they...?

In the upper part of Vasari's fresco, a soldier waves a green flag with the words "cerca trova" ("He who seeks, finds"). It is thought by some to hint that the lost da Vinci painting "The Battle of Anghiari" may be hidden someplace nearby.

PLACES ~ GEMS

Ornately decorated ceiling inside the palace.

As you wander through the historic district, you will find the Palazzo Vecchio, recognizable by her lanky crenellated tower that hovers over the Piazza della Signoria. To enter, ascend the few steps between the imposing statues of "David" and "Hercules & Cacus" and you will find yourself on the ground floor of the Palazzo Vecchio.

You can wander in for free and be immediately rewarded by this marvellously frescoed room - or lobby. Verrocchio's delightful "Putto with Dolphin" will amuse you from the center fountain

as you inspect the surrounding walls. You will find some faded old paintings of the way Florence looked at different points throughout history.

Then hang out in the corner of the room for a couple of minutes, and feel the drama that permeates these ancient walls: can you 'hear' the ancient speeches echoing in your mind? Or 'see' the 15th century city officials giving orders to the armor-clad guards? Or notice the whispering among the local citizens as they plan a secret Medici over-throw?

When you have finished with this room, go over to the next room, buy a ticket and treat yourself to the rest of this historically charged architectural marvel.

Constructed by Arnolfo di Cambio in 1299, Palazzo Vecchio *("Old Palace")* has seen many iterations. *And oh, if those walls could speak...!*

- It was originally built to accommodate the Priori and the Gonfaloniere di Giustizia, or the Justices
- It has acted as a Sheriff's office and a prison
- During the 14th century, the Medici used this building to accommodate the city officials giving them a sizeable arena that could handle the increasingly complex civic issues
- A palace with secret doors and chambers which allowed 'certain guests' to come and go without being seen
- A hideaway for a later somewhat reclusive Medici Duke (Franchesco 1)
- A Museum - today

This barrel-shaped room was created by Giorgio Vasari for the shy and awkward Duke, Franchesco 1 de' Medici. Many of the lower panels will open to reveal closets that once stored valuable pieces of art. The paintings gave clues as to the contents of each. One panel opens to a secret passageway to...?

The (real!) funerary death mask of Dante Alighieri, similar to the one described in Dan Brown's well-loved novel "Inferno" can be found within the Palazzo .

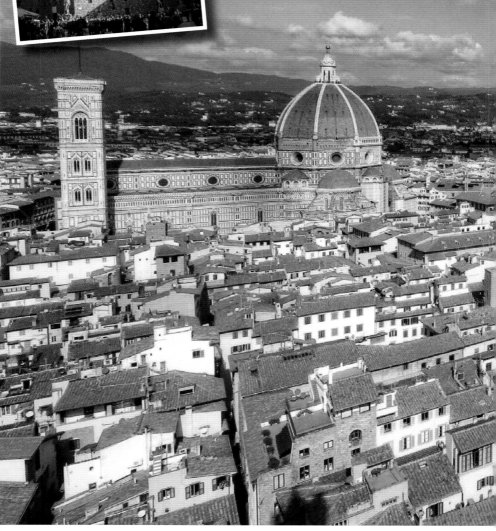

Palazzo Vecchio

The Stairway to Hell (for some)

While visiting this historically-charged city, climbing the tower of the Palazzo Vecchio is a must-do activity. As you climb this famous tower, you will pass a small prison cell that once held Cosimo (the Elder) Medici, and coincidentally enough, some 50 years later it held a famous Medici enemy, Girolamo Savonarola - the despised friar that

GEMS ~ PLACES

created the Bonfire of the Vanities that consumed the art of some of the most beloved painters such as Sandro Botticelli.

Upon reaching the top of the tower, you will be treated to one of the most spectacular views of the city around all four sides of this crenellated tower. The climb is definitely worth the effort!

PLACES ~ GEMS

PONTE VECCHIO

OLD BRIDGE

Ponte Vecchio Trivia

1. The Ponte Vecchio was the only bridge to be spared by the Nazi bombing in 1944.
2. There are over 50 jewelry stores on this venerable bridge today.
3. Most of the jewelry stores have been handed down from generation to generation for many years
4. The mysterious **Vasari Corridor** runs over the TOP of the Ponte Vecchio.
5. The Ponte Vecchio is said to be the most photographed bridge in the world.
   6. If you throw a key from the Ponte Vecchio, your love will be eternal.

GEMS ~ PLACES

VIETATO APPORRE LUCCHETTI
ALLA RECINZIONE E AL MONUMENTO
IN BASE ALL 'ART. 112 DEL REGOLAMENTO DI POLIZIA MUNICIPALE

SANZIONE PREVISTA €160.00.

IT'S NOT ALLOWED TO HANG LOCKS
ON THE RAILING

AS IT IS RULED BY THE RULE OF MUNICIPAL POLICE ARTART. 112

FINE €160.00 TO TRASGRESSORS.

The Legend of the Locks

It is said that if you put a lock on the Ponte Vecchio bridge and throw the key into the waters below, your love will be eternal.

(Hmm, too bad it's not legal, right?)

The view from the inside of the Vasari Corridor looking down on to the Ponte Vecchio: halfway across the bridge is a fenced-in statue of Cellini. In the distance is the Ponte Santa Trinita bridge and behind that, the Ponte Carraia bridge.

"PONTE VECCHIO" [PON-ta VEK-yo]
"Old Bridge"

This famous bridge with its storied past was originally built during the Dark Ages around the year 990. It was washed away in 1117, rebuilt, washed away again in 1333, and again rebuilt. It is the only remaining bridge in Florence after all of the others were destroyed by Hitler's forces during WWII. But it still boasts some of the original underwater supporting structures, and one of the old watch towers still stands on the south end of the bridge.

The Ponte Vecchio is the only remaining bridge in Florence after all of the others were destroyed by Hitler's forces during WWII.

The Ponte Vecchio connects the northern touristic and the business sections of Florence with her southern more residential areas, separated by the **Arno River**.

During the Renaissance period, the shops contained many types of food-supplying places, such as fresh fruit stands, meat markets, butcheries, eateries, etc. Running along the top of the Ponte Vecchio is the Vasari Corridor, the secret above-ground tunnel build for Cosimo I de' Medici, the Grand Duke of Tuscany. (Late Renaissance.)

The Ponte Vecchio is also known as the Gold Bridge because this tiny bridge is solidly lined on both sides with over 50 upscale jewelry stores. Never will you see so much bling on one tiny bridge anywhere in the world.

The **Grand Duke**, who walked over the bridge inside the Corridor daily, ordered all of the stinky food shops on the bridge to be replaced with shops that would not produce such a vile stench to his ever-so-delicate nostrils. He ordered that the bridge be filled with shops that were worthy of being walked over by his very important and illustrious guests. The results are the many beautiful jewelry shops spanning both sides of the bridge today.

Giorgio Vasari, for whom the Corridor was named, was an artist by trade, but he is more widely remembered as an architect. For not only did he design the Corridor, he was also the genius behind the most visited museum in the world: the **Uffizi Gallery.**

On many evenings you will find local musicians performing everything from classic Italian opera to your favorite Rock & Roll. American music is loved everywhere throughout Italy.

So when the sun goes down, take a stroll on to the Ponte Vecchio to watch these talented performers, while the glistening **Arno** flows gently below your feet.

PITTI PALACE
SIX MUSEUMS IN ONE LITTLE PALAZZO

The Pitti Palace was originally designed by Filippo Brunelleschi in the mid-1400's for a local Florentine banker named Luca Pitti. Pitti wanted a home that was larger than any other home in the area - especially one that would outshine the home of his powerful enemies, the Medici. A century after Pitti's death, Cosimo I de' Medici purchased the property, expanded it significantly, and made sure that all of the Pitti crests and markings were replaced by Medici symbols. *(Actually, his wife Eleanora of Toledo purchased it; she couldn't possibly raise her future royal children in their current little Medici Villa. Sniff!)*

All Pitti banners were removed except one: while the Grand Duke did remove it from the Palace, he moved it to the corner of a small building across the street so that it could spend eternity having to stare at the home that was transformed into the palace you see today by his Medici rival.

Over the centuries this beautiful home became the power center for all Florentine leaders, including Napoleon in the 1800's. And in 1944 it acted as a shelter to thousands of people who were evacuated from their homes along the Arno River during the Nazi bombings.

Today, the Pitti Palace is home to some of the most important pieces of art in Tuscany, and includes six separate galleries to display the porcelain, costumes, silver, sculptures and paintings of the time.

BOBOLI GARDENS
THE LONE GREEN SPOT

GEMS ~ PLACES

The Fountain of Neptune is nicknamed the "Fountain of the Fork" by the local Florentines.

Throughout the Boboli Gardens, you will find miles of paths, an unexpected collection of sculptures, shady areas, benches, and grassy lawns. Each area seems to have its own theme. Some areas have been landscaped into mazes, which make it fun to simply wander. You'll never know where you'll end up! There are even plenty of tiny hideouts to enjoy a quiet picnic with a friend. And because there are a variety of hills throughout the Gardens, you will be treated to a variety of vistas of the city.

Reale Giardino di Boboli

Some areas of the Gardens have been cleverly landscaped into patterns that are pleasing to the eye.

This Egyptian Obelisk was brought to the gardens from the Villa Medici in Rome.

The Boboli Gardens were added to the Pitti Palace by Eleonora de' Medici. She wished to have a place where the Medici family could ride their horses for pleasure without having to go out to the main streets with the rabble. In addition, Cosimo I & Leonora bore 11 children that needed a safe backyard in which to play.

The term 'Garden' may conjure up images of manually-planted flowers. Lots of them. Boboli Gardens will not fulfil those images, as there are very few flowers in this huge outdoor green area. Boboli Gardens more resembles a cluster of parks all strung together. Given that, the grounds are huge and beautiful. It is fun to select a path and take it wherever it leads. There are beautiful monuments, statues and other surprises to be found in nearly every crack, crevice and clearing.

The Gardens have been creatively landscaped, and in most areas, they have preserved the natural flow of the land.

If a picnic is what you have in mind, there is a delicatessen in the Palazzo Pitti Courtyard where you will find plenty of picnic goodies to suit your appetite. From there, exit the courtyard to proceed directly out back to the Gardens. Do not stop under the first tree you find, as a little exploration will yield a wide variety of shady choices and views from which you can enjoy your outing in the sunshine.

Hidden in the Garden is this ancient-looking bronze sculpture created in 1998 by artist Igor Mitoraj. It is titled "Tindaro Screpolato" meaning, appropriately, "Cracked Face."

187

GROTTO DI BUONTALENTI
PRISONERS IN THE WALLS

GEMS ~ PLACES

The Exterior of the Grotto di Buontalenti.

Hidden in Boboli Gardens

A stroll through the northwest sector of the Gardens will yield to an unconventional-looking structure that appears as though a child carelessly threw mud up against a building in an angry fit. This unique style is that of artist Bernardo Buontalenti who was a favored artist of Francesco I de' Medici (son of Cosimo I). Intended as an artist's interpretation of a real cave or grotto, it boasts three rooms in succession commonly seen in mannerist-style architecture.

If you look closely, the rugged-looking edges look like they were made from sea shells & mud to form the stalactites (1). This little building contains three small rooms within it, two with sculptures. In the exterior 'cave' (2, 4, 5, 6, 7) there are forms of people seeping out from the walls. (3) shows the gorgeous frescoes on the walls & ceiling. From this angle you can see the two inner rooms. One contains "Paris and Helen" by Vincenzo de' Rossi, and the other houses Giambologna's "Bathing Venus" surrounded by frescos. This Grotto was started by **Vasari** *then completed by Buontalenti. It is meant to depict a shelter for shepherds.*

1

2

3

"Grotto di Madama" with its own ornate ceiling. This Grotto is in the main building, and there is yet another - the "Adam & Eve Grotto" - in the outlaying area of the gardens. Have I missed any? Have you? ▶

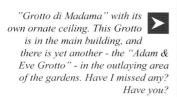

In Dan Brown's best-selling novel "Inferno," Robert Langdon and Sienna hid from the police in the Grotto di Buontalenti.

4

Buontalenti's Grottos emit a sense of eeriness as these seemingly imprisoned people try to escape these walls. It is somewhat reminiscent of Michelangelo's "Slaves" *in the* Accademia.

5   6   7

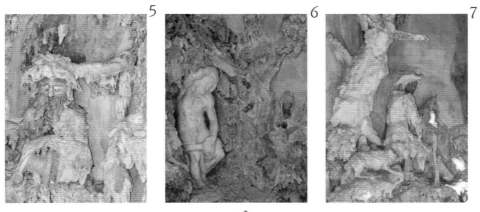

PLACES ~ GEMS

BASILICA DI SAN LORENZO
A MICHELANGELO MASTERPIECE
Piazza di San Lorenzo, 9, 50123 Firenze

Originally consecrated in 393 by the Bishop of Milan, the Basilica di San Lorenzo was reconstructed in 1059. The Medici family hired Filippo Brunelleschi to again rebuild it in 1418. Throughout the following decades, some of the most famous Renaissance artists were hired to add their own creative touches. This included Donatello, Filippo Lippi, Ghirlandaio and Verrocchio. In the early 1500's, Michelangelo was brought in to design the facades, to build the new sacristy and to add the exquisite Laurentian Library. The Church of St. Lawrence is considered to be the crown representative of Florentine Renaissance Architecture that still remains intact today.

Pope Leo X (son of Lorenzo the Magnificent), hired Michelangelo *to design the exterior façade. For the original design sketches, Michelangelo designed everything according to the proportions of the ideal human body* (Vitruvian Man). *He used those sketches to create this wooden model. Unfortunately his façade was never completed. Michelangelo did, however, successfully design the internal façade.*

Filippo Brunelleschi died before the completion of the Basilica. Other designers (possibly Michelozzo or Manetti) finished the building, losing many of Brunelleschi's original design concepts.

MEDICI CHAPEL

Inside, the "Chapel of the Princes"
boasts of royal opulence. Cosimo I
de' Medici, the Grand Duke of Tuscany,
conceived of the idea of creating a chapel
that would be splendiferous enough to
house the Medici 'Princes' for all of eternity. Nearly every surface has been inlaid
with marbles and granites acquired from a
myriad of Italian quarries. The completed
design was a result of a collaboration of
designers and architects that took several
generations to finish. The tombs of the
various Medici can be found around the
room, and an assortment of Medici coats
of arms have been incorporated into the
design as well.

Hiding Michelangelo

In fear for his life, Michelangelo
hid for three months in a small
secret chamber under the Medici
Chapel. See "Michelangelo's
Hideaway *p122*

The Tomb of Lorenzo (il Magnifico) de' Medici was created lovingly by Michelangelo for his patron and dear friend. The two sculptures in front represent Dawn and Dusk.

The Tomb of Lorenzo's cherished brother Giuliano de' Medici was also created by Michelangelo. The two sculptures in front represent Day and Night.

191

LAURENTIAN LIBRARY
A MICHELANGELO MASTERPIECE
Piazza San Lorenzo, 9, 50123 Firenze, Telephone +39 055 210760

The Laurentian Library is a lesser-known display of Michelangelo's indisputable architectural genius. It was Pope Clement VII (Giulio de' Medici, son of Giuliano di Piero de' Medici) who hired **Michelangelo** to create this stunning home for Cosimo (the Elder) Medici's unprecedented and treasured collection of ancient books and manuscripts.

Michelangelo spent nearly ten arduous years personally involved with this project, including the time he spent creating the initial drawings for this spectacular tribute to his beloved Medici family. Giorgio Vasari and Bartolomeo Ammannati were chosen to finish the building because of their strict and non-variant adherence to Michelangelo's original drawings and wishes. Michelangelo continued revisiting its progress between his trips to Rome.

For Michelangelo fans, the Laurentian Library is a must-see. Located conveniently next to the

The steps into the Laurentian Library are an original use of stacked ovals creating a grand and graceful introduction to Michelangelo's *architectural masterpiece.*

Cappella de' Medici (Medici Chapel), it is one of the more beautiful (and lesser known) of the many museums that you will find in Florence.

Upon entering from the Brunelleschi cloister, you will notice how Michelangelo used 'ovals' stacked upon one another to form the grand entry staircase (far left). The curves of the steps are accentuated greatly by the straight lines that cover the walls and shoot straight up to that exquisitely adorned high ceiling,
itself stunning in its simple symmetry.

Michelangelo put his heart into every single detail from the floors to the intricately carved ceilings, and from the stained glass windows to the actual height and size of the desks themselves.
Once inside, you will see a masterpiece of symmetry that leads your eye first to the far end of this expansive room, over to the beautifully ornate windows (replete with images of the familiar Medici coat of arms), then lastly, to the pew-like rows of seats. Topping off the room is that intricately perfect ceiling that makes one feel truly humbled in the stalwartness created by the rhythmically arranged lines and patterns far overhead.

Inside the Tribune of Elci, a small room adjacent to the Main hall, the decorous and dominant dome defines the shape of the room that is echoed in the intricate patterns on the floor. Today this room is used as a study room for workshops.

PLACES ~ GEMS

GEMS ~ PLACES

Because there were only a few hundred printed books at that time, they were all placed on the desks, and chained down to prevent theft. When someone wanted to see a particular book, they would simply look at the titles and descriptions attached to the end of each row of seats until they found the desired book.

Today the library is home to over 11,000 manuscripts and 4,500 early-printed books, the single-most prestigious collection in all of Italy.

The Library is the single most perfect example of the sheer genius of Michelangelo, not just as a painter and a sculptor, but as an architect par excellence!

After visiting the Library, one must ask themselves how Michelangelo could have designed this stunning structure with so little architectural experience behind him. Besides this Laurentian Library, and the Medici Chapel, Michelangelo was also chiefly involved in the redesign of the truly magnificent St. Peter's Basilica in Rome. Wow!

The Laurentian Library is often missed even by the most ardent fans of Michelangelo and the Medici, and if you have not considered following either of them, seeing this building will surely make a fan out of you.

Along the walls of the main library hall are the stained glass windows decorated with a variety of symbols important to the Medici family with the famous balled crest featured in its center. If you look closely at each of them, you'll be able to differentiate the glass that has been newly created, from the windows that still remain intact from antiquity.

In the cavernous main hall you will see that each bench is labelled with the titles of the books that were located in that row. All you had to do was to find the row where your book of interest was located, and slide in (pew-like). There were very few books during that time, and there was usually only a single copy of a book in existence. So each book was chained to the desks to prevent removal. If you wished to see another book, you had to relocate yourself to another row, and another seat.

PLACES ~ GEMS

BARGELLO
A DARK AND DISMAL PAST

GEMS ~ PLACES

PLACES ~ GEMS

The courtyard within the walls of the Bargello has seen many
forms of punishment and torture throughout its history. Grizzly
executions occurred until 1876 when Pietro Leopoldo, the Grand Duke
of Tuscany, abolished executions as a means of punishment.
When you walk through this courtyard, you will know that you are
stepping on the blood of the many souls who were put to death in
this violence-charged building.

Built in 1255, the Bargello was originally intended to be the office for the 'Chief of Police', or the 'Capitan del Popolo' *(the Captain of the People)*, and is today the oldest public building in Florence. The term 'Bargello' is derived from the Latin meaning 'fortified tower.' Over the years, it has been known by various names that include the Bargello Palace, Palazzo del Podestà, Museo Nazionale del Bargello, or Palazzo del Popolo *(Palace of the People)*. It has been a barracks, a prison and an office of justice. Today it is a National Museum that houses an impressive collection of sculptures, ceramics, coins, textiles, tapestries, wax, silver and ironworks. Take notice of the two Davids: one sculpted by Verrocchio and the other sculpted by Donatello *(p128)*. Each artist had his own 'take' on the famous story of David and Goliath, evident in each of their sculptures. These Davids were quite famous for decades before Michelangelo put a chisel to stone to create his epic version of David. In addition, you will see the shiny and colorful works in porcelain by della Robbia, a local artist favored by Cosimo I de' Medici, the Grand Duke of Tuscany.

Michelangelo's "Drunken Bacchus" is a popular resident of the Bargello. ▼

Sculpture by Bartolomeo Ammannati, originally designed for the Sala Grande in the Palazzo Vecchio, *now resides at the Bargello. The influence of ancient Rome & Greece is apparent in this piece.* ▼

Goddess Juno

Personification of the Arno River

Ceres, Goddess of Agriculture

Prudence with anchor and dolphin, symbols of Cosimo I of Florence

Fountain of Parnassus with Pegasus

Flora as the personification of Florence

The Bargello is easily seen in the historic district of Florence. The distinct crenellated roof and bell tower make it easy to identify in the city skyline. Crenellations were created so that guns and cannons could be placed on the rooftop while still possessing a modicum of protection for the soldier. It is told that during the Renaissance, people would look up from the streets and see bodies hanging - sometimes upside down - from these crenellations. This was intended to warn others to beware of the punishment of serious crimes and treason against the current ruler or body of government.

PLACES ~ GEMS

Originally created as a fountain figure at the House of Medici, Giambologna's bronze "Mercury" holding a caduceus (now used as a symbol for medicine) can be seen in the Bargello Museum. It is considered to be of the 'Mannerist' style, as it's elongated form can be viewed from all sides.

Sculpture of Cosimo I de' Medici by Baccio Bandinelli - 1539

Both of these exquisite bronze David statues were created - and famous - long before Michelangelo created his own globally-cherished version of David. They can be found in the Bargello Museum. Left: Donatello's David. Right: Verrocchio's David.

199

VASARI CORRIDOR
THE MYSTERIOUS PASSAGEWAY OF POWER

During the Middle Ages, it was not possible for a ruler to walk down the street like a normal person without the looming fear of being murdered. **Cosimo I de' Medici** was no different, as his band of guards surrounded him though still he feared for his life during his journey to work and home each and every day. So he asked his friend and favorite architect Giorgio Vasari what it would take to build a private passageway that would take him in safety between his home at the Pitti Palace and his work at the Palazzo Vecchio. He was not interested in skulking through an underground tunnel like a coward each day; rather he wanted Vasari to build an overhead passageway that would be seen as a symbol of power rather than one of fear.

Vasari had his hands full with this request. He had to figure out how to get Medici to the river, across the shop-jammed bridge, past what is now the Uffizi Gallery, then terminate at the Palazzo Vecchio. But overhead? It would be impossible to tear down every structure along the way, as these were the homes and businesses of so many of their prominent citizens. He had to devise a clever way to build over the top of all of them! And to make matters worse, Cosimo I wanted it 'yesterday.'

Vasari was indeed successful in creating this overhead corridor for his Medici boss. But not only did he complete it in a satisfactory manner, he finished it in an astonishing six months, much to the delight of his esteemed superior, Cosimo I de' Medici, the Grand Duke of Tuscany.

The corridor starts at the Pitti Palace, passes through a church where the family could secretly attend Mass, and it continues to cross the river riding on the top of the Ponte Vecchio (bridge), then snakes through and past a few buildings including the Uffizi Gallery to terminate at the Palazzo Vecchio.

Pitti Palace *(home)*

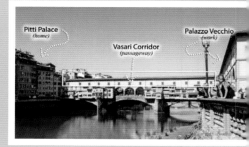

|<---- The Vasari Corridor is approxir

The Vasari Corridor winds its way over the top of the city connecting the Pitti Palace with the Palazzo Vecchio. Today it is lined with the world's largest collection of self-portraits. Visitors cannot traverse the Corridor alone. Due to the fragility of the art, visitors must be closely accompanied by a licensed guide.

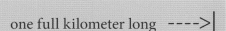
one full kilometer long ---->|

Palazzo Vecchio *(work)*

Vasari Corridor

Cosimo I de' Medici, the Grand duke of Tuscany, often used the Vasari Corridor to escort his important guests safely through town. But it stunk of butchered meats and rotten vegetables. So he ordered that all food be removed from the corridor, and replaced with something more befitting of the delicate nostrils of his esteemed guests. Always wishing to please the Grand Duke, the merchants chucked the beef (☺) and replaced the food vendors with fine gold and jewelry shops. Today there are nearly 50 jewelry stores on this tiny bridge. *(p180)*

Today with its seemingly unending wall space, the Vasari Corridor is lined with some of the Uffizi's overflow of art that includes the largest collection of self-portraits in the world.

This view from inside of the Vasari Corridor secretly looks down over the heads of the tourists as they shop for gold jewelry on the famous Ponte Vecchio bridge.

Between the Pitti Palace and the Ponte Vecchio, you will find the Piazza di San Felice. The Vasari Corridor passes right by the San Felice Church with an opening that enabled the Medici family to attend mass on a private loge safely and unnoticed above and behind the public pews. Afterwards, they would simply step back into the above-ground corridor and continue to the office or to home.

SANTA CROCE
WHERE THE BODIES ARE BURIED

◀ *The Church of Santa Croce dominates the neighborhood.*

Dante Alighieri stands vigil outside of Santa Croce. ▶

Santa Croce, besides currently offering full religious services, is the resting place for some of the most notable people from the Renaissance era and later.

This is a Franciscan Church and a Basilica of the Roman Catholic Church. It is located in the Piazza di Santa Croce: a few blocks east of the Palazzo Vecchio, and a few blocks north of the Ponte alle Grazie Bridge.

Nicolò Matas, a Jewish architect, designed the church's neo-gothic facade, making sure to include a large Star of David at the top of the main frontal facade. Matas had wanted to be buried with his peers but because he was Jewish, he was buried under the porch and not inside the building.

As are all of the other churches and cathedrals in this city, Santa Croce will not disappoint! It is daunting to absorb its enormity in a single glance, so taking it one step at a time is highly advised.

Walking through this cavernous tribute to God, you will come across the tombs of some of the most famous people in the history of Florence and of the world: Galileo, Michelangelo, Cellini, Botticelli, and the Pazzi family, to name only a few. Many of the tombs are not just famous because of their residents: they were also designed and created by some of the world's most renowned artists, like Donatello for example. Although da Vinci did not spend much time in this city, Florence nevertheless claims him as one of their own because of the work he did in Florence during his formative years, and his obvious influence on the success of the Renaissance in general. A tributary tomb in da Vinci's honor can be seen in the Church of Santa Croce even though he is actually entombed in France's Chapel Saint-Hubert.

16 CHAPELS

If you had a lot of money, an interior private chapel could be dedicated in your name, such as the chapels of the Medici and the Bonaparte families.

Giotto's paintings are beautifully displayed in many of the alcoves throughout the church. A surprising collection of shiny clay statuary created by locally famous artists from the della Robbia family are scattered throughout. In addition you will find an excellent collection of works by Donatello, Cimabue and Vasari, among others. In an outdoor courtyard, a statuary tribute to Florence Nightingale *(named after her parents' favorite city)* is mounted to a wall.

Outside, the Piazza di Santa Croce is quite spacious and is lined with outdoor dining places, leather shops and umbrellaed souvenir booths. You will almost certainly find some form of live entertainment on most any afternoon in the spacious and often crowded Piazza di Santa Croce.

A monumental tribute to Florence Nightingale can be found outside in the main cloister.

These are the tombs for Dante Alighieri, Michelangelo *and* Galileo *respectively. The intricate detail and care in their creations speak to the tremendous imprints they each left on Florence.*

MUSEO GALILEO
A BEAUTIFUL MIND, A BEAUTIFUL MAN
Piazza dei Giudici, 1, 50122 Firenze

"All truths are easy to understand once they are discovered; the point is to discover them." ~ Galileo Galilei

Galileo's obsession with both time and space led him to the ability to measure distances accurately. He either invented or improved on a wide variety of instruments and tools of science and measurement, like the compass, the sextant, the telescope and the microscope, among a plethora of others.

With these implements, one could measure both the sizes and distances of planets, as well as the speed at which they travel on their orbital paths. By determining 'longitude,' he could help sailors to calculate their current location at any point in the oceans and to navigate to anywhere around the world. The ability to measure distance and perspective (via triangulation) is - even today - useful in the design of roads and buildings.

The Museo Galileo is arranged in 18 rooms, on two floors. The rooms on the first floor exhibit items from the Medici collections, and the rooms on the second floor exhibit items from the Lorraine collections as follows:

First Floor Rooms

1 - The Medici Collections

2 - Astronomy and Time

3 - The Representation of the World

4 - Vincenzo Coronelli's Globes

5 - The Science of Navigation

6 - The Science of Warfare

7 - Galileo's New World

8 - "The Accademia del Cimento"
   The Art & Science of Experimentation

9 - After Galileo:
   Exploring the Physical and Biological Worlds

Second Floor Rooms

10 - The Lorraine Collections

11 - The Spectacle of Science

12 - Teaching & Popularizing Science: Mechanics

13 - Teaching & Popularizing Science: Optics, Pheumatics, Electromagnetism

14 - The Precision Instrument Industry

15 - Measuring Natural Phenomena: Atmosphere and Light

16 - Measuring Natural Phenomena: Electricity and Electromagnetism

17 - Chemistry and the Public Usefulness of Science

18 - Science in the Home

"I have never met a man so ignorant that I couldn't learn something from him." ~ Galileo Galilei

The Armillary Sphere represents our solar system as understood by Aristotle and later refined by Ptolemy. It depicts the Earth-centric orbital path of the planets. Galileo, however, realized that in actuality, the planets (including Earth) all rotate around the Sun. Note the ever-present Medici Coat of Arms just left of the center of the sphere.

GEMS ~ PLACES

da VINCI MUSEUM
A TRIBUTE TO LEONARDO
Via dei Servi, 66, 50100 Firenze

"Glider" The wings, similar to those of large birds, are fixed to the centre of the craft, while the pilot commands the extremities by means of a cable. (MacchineDiLeonardo.com)

This machine resembles his ornithopter, a flying machine with bird wings: A set of belts tie the pilot, supine, on a wooden surface. The pilot pushes the pedals with his feet, thus setting the wings in motion.

This is a model of da Vinci's concept for a machine gun.

Finding da Vinci Today

Leonardo da Vinci Museum

Address: Via dei Servi, 66, 50100 Firenze, Italy
Descendants of da Vinci have painstakingly recreated life-sized versions of Leonardo's machines and inventions like the ones seen on these pages.

The Uffizi Gallery:

The Uffizi proudly dedicates a room to da Vinci. In it you will find several of his paintings, including the "Annunciation" and "The Baptism of Christ" which he created with Maestro Verrocchio.

Outside the Uffizi Gallery:

You will find a statue of Leonardo among the outdoor gallery of greats.

Online

http://www.MacchineDiLeonardo.com
A wonderful website that boasts da Vinci's marvellous inventions ~ and his mind.

An online tour of the Da Vinci Halls Artwork within the Uffizi Museum can be found at
http://www.VirtualUffizi.com/leonardo-da-vinci.html

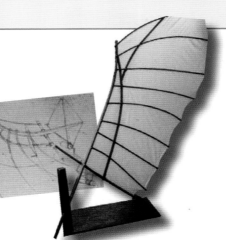

PLACES ~ GEMS

CONVENT of SAN MARCO
CONVENT AND MUSEUM
Piazza San Marco, 3, 50121 Firenze

In 1436, Cosimo (the Elder) de' Medici, as a ruler of the city, decided to take this fought-over eye-sore and turn it into a proper church. He hired the architect **Michelozzo**, the same gifted architect that designed the Medici home in the middle of the city, to come and fix this time-worn old structure. Once completed, he brought in his favorite painter, the immensely popular Fra Angelico. Angelico was an exceptionally talented painter with a happy disposition. He worked fast, and he was really good.

In the design of the building, Michelozzo included a library, understated in its elegance *(below)*, that became a common destination for Medici and his cronies to hang out and discuss the problems of the world. Or at least those that plagued

Michelozzo, Cosimo de' Medici's favorite architect, designed this convent for his chief patron. He included a beautiful library for Cosimo. This was Europe's first public library.

Fra Angelico was hired by Cosimo de' Medici to decorate this convent. He was a sweet demure man, who is so revered even today for the abundance of art he left for us to enjoy.

Cosimo (the Elder) de' Medici, shrewd in his business dealings, was the savvy and wealthy banker that purchased the convent of San Marco for renovation.

Fra Girolamo Savonarola lived here as a friar for 10+ years. He eventually became prior for San Marco. This is where he lived when the authorities came to arrest him for his execution.

Florence. In addition to the stately library, Michelozzo added a small chamber cell where Cosimo could sneak away to get some quality alone time. It was here that 50 years later, **Fra Girolamo Savonarola**, an outspoken enemy of the Medici, lived for several years before the men in uniform bodily removed him (and two of his most ardent followers), from the premises. This was the event that did not end not well for Savonarola, as he was ultimately marched onto a platform (in the same spot where he forced citizens to burn their art and personal belongings) from which he was first hanged, then burned at the stake in an ironic version of his own "Bonfire of the Vanities."

Original Graffiti

As you wander through Florence, you may see some buildings that seem to be overly decorated on the outside. It almost seems as though they are wearing a delicate lacy veil around them. Back in the old days, this was a style of external decoration that was intended to dress-up the finest buildings. This style was known as "Graffiti".

PLACES ~ GEMS

ORSANMICHELE
THE OLD GRANARY
Via dell'Arte della Lana, 50123 Firenze

Halfway between the Duomo and the Palazzo Vecchio lies an old building that seems to be a bit out of place as you shop your way through the touristic historic district of Florence. This building, called Orsanmichele, is one of the oldest buildings in town. It was originally built to replace a Benedictine convent and its orchards in the 8th century to serve as an Oratory *(prayer chapel)* for San Michele *(Saint Michael)*. It burned down and was later rebuilt using stone and bricks in the 1200's by Arnolfo di Cambio to be used as a grain market. The lower floor was used to keep wheat on-hand for easy transport to the straw market one block away. The upper area was used to store grain; two of the large pillars were used to move the grain between the floors. On one of the pillars within this granary, there existed an image of the Madonna del Popolo ~ Madonna of the People. In 1348 the Black Death *(an extremely lethal strain of the bubonic plague)* reduced the considerable local population from well over 100,000 to less than 40,000 citizens who relied on this Madonna to provide cures, and would come and say an extra prayer to encourage good health and healing. Apparently this worked because the plague eventually dissipated and the devotion to this work was escalated to new heights. The legend of the powers of the Madonna grew and an ornate tabernacle was constructed to enshrine and protect the venerated painting. This Madonna was now one of the most revered pieces of art in the city, and it garnered enough charitable contributions to enable more 'upgrades.'

The building itself served a dual purpose as a place of worship and a grain market. In the early 1400's, the architect Simone Talenti redesigned the ground floor as a church, and in the two upper two floors, citizens stored wheat. This was in the event there was an attack and they couldn't get to the fields, or there were weather issues like floods or droughts in the farmlands.

The trade guilds used the building primarily as a chapel. Niches were created around the exterior of the building, and at

The original fresco of the Madonna was later replaced by another Madonna that held curative powers for the local citizens. The Madonna became so revered that they built this tabernacle around her to both honor her and to protect her.

a time when the desire for artists and sculptors was in high demand, the controlling Silk Guild decided to fill the niches with sculptures representing the patron saint of each guild.

Recently, the city has cast reproductions of these sculptures to replace the originals in the exterior niches. The originals were cleaned and restored, and can now be seen on the upper floor in the Gallery that was created to protect them from any further harm from the elements.

Point to Ponder

Who invented that cold gelato that you might be enjoying right now? All over Italy, many cities claim 'ownership' of that refreshing coneful of yum. Here in Florence, as the story goes, a guy named Bernardo Buontalenti invented it for *Cosimo I de' Medici* to celebrate the Spanish Deputation. Buontalenti, a self-proclaimed inventor of pretty much everything, did also create the grottos in the *Boboli Gardens*, Forte Belvedere, and the tribune in the Uffizi Gallery.

Things to Notice

- Exterior niches containing the patron Saint of each of the Guilds *(next page)*
- The round disks made of the new material: a shiny ceramic - with colour (very unusual for any kind of statuary of the day)
- The slots in two of the interior pillars where the grain would pass are still present
- Climb the spiral staircase that goes to what is now a gallery; it used to be the upper floor that held the grain

Orsanmichele

As you walk around the exterior of Orsanmichele (the granary turned church), you will see several round emblems overhead. With the exception of the Butchers' Guild emblem (made by the Ginori Porcelain Mfg), the emblems were created by Lucca della Robbia, an artist that utilized as his medium his own newly created material, a cross between ceramic and porcelain. Like the larger sculptures in the niches, each emblem represents an individual guild. Glazed works were not only unique at that point in history, but they were also well-suited to withstand the potential of harsh weather conditions.

| *Silk Guild* | *Physicians/ Apoth-ecaries Guild* | *Butchers Guild* | *Stone & Wood Carvers Guild* | *Symbol of Florence* |

"Madonna and Child"
by Tedesco for the Doctors & Apothocaries Guild

"Four Saints"
By Banco for the Wood and Stone Guilds

"St. Mark"
by Donatello for the Linen Weavers & Peddlers

"St. Philip"
by Banco for the Shoemakers Guild

"Christ St. Thomas"
by Verrocchio for the Merchants Guild

"St. Eligius"
by Banco for the
Arte dei Maniscalchi

"St. James"
by Lamaberti for the
Furriers Guild

"St. Peter"
by Brunelleschi for the
Butchers Guild

"St. John the Baptist"
by Ghiberti for the
Calimala Merchants Guild

"St. George"
by Donatello for the
Armorers Guild

"St. Matthew"
by Ghiberti for the
Bankers Guild

"St. Stephen"
by Ghiberti for the
Wool Manufacturers Guild

"St. John the Evangelist"
by Montelupo for the
Silk Merchants Guild

"St. Luke"
by Giambologna for the
Magisters and Notaries Guild

PLACES ~ GEMS

215

BRANCACCI CHAPEL
WALLS OF MASACCIO
Cappella Brancacci, Piazza del Carmine, 50124 Firenz

Inside of the **Church of Santa Maria del Carmine** is the ornately decorated Brancacci Chapel (Cappella dei Brancacci). Constructed in 1268, it appears startlingly plain in contrast to the many ornate churches seen today throughout Florence. That most of the original church and its artwork were destroyed in a fire in 1771 explains this fact. But, somehow, two chapels remained intact after the fire: The Corsini Chapel and the Brancacci Chapel.

Masaccio, one of the 5 original great artists who unknowingly launched the Renaissance art movement, and whose frescoes line the walls of the chapel, was one of the first artists (in 1,000 years) to create the human body in its nude form. He was revered for his foreshortening (use of linear perspective) of the figures in his scenes to depict distance. And from his friend Filippo Brunelleschi (another of the original five Renaissance initiators), he learned to apply linear perspective to architecture. Two excellent examples of these techniques can be found in the Brancacci Chapel.

b.   *a.*   *c.*

▲ **"Tribute of Money"** *by Masaccio ~ 1425*

a: *Depicted in the main scene is Christ surrounded by his Apostles (each with a halo) who are met by a tax collector (the man dressed in an orange tunic, facing away - with no halo). Christ has no money with which to pay a tax, which shows on the concerned faces of his Apostles. Christ, knowing that a miracle will take care of this issue, points to St. Peter gesturing him to get money from the fish in the water "over there."*

b: *St. Peter, after doffing his orange robe, bends down into the river and opens the mouth of the fish in order to retrieve money from its stomach.*

c: *St. Peter, redressed in his robes, hands the money to the tax collector.*

Masaccio's use of light and shadow lends a strong sense of realism to the scene. The center point of linear perspective is on Christ's face. The lines in the architecture of the building clarify the joining of those invisible perspective lines. Masaccio infused a palette of grays to depict the far away distant mountains.

The Fig Leaf

The idea of using the Fig Leaf as a means of cover originated in biblical times. Adam and Eve, in order to hide their shame after biting the forbidden apple, used a fig leaf to cover their nudity, hence their shame. Throughout history, the fig leaf has been used metaphorically to illustrate shame, a secret or a cover-up.

Throughout the post-Renaissance centuries, the acceptance of nude art came and went. Fig leaves were commonly sculpted, carved, or painted to convert improper nude art into more acceptable exhibits. In some instances, the attempts to remove an add-on fig leaf created even more damage to the original work of art.

The removal of fig leaves from artwork today still causes protest among the general population. One side wishes to re-expose the original work of art as intended and created by the original artist. While the other side, believing that even though a fig leaf was added later, it still must be considered art in itself and should not be removed or destroyed.

Her Royally Embarrassed Highness

Near the end of his rule in 1568, **Cosimo I de' Medici**, the Grand Duke of Tuscany, had a duplicate cast of **Michelangelo's "David"** created as a gift to Queen Victoria. Appalled by the brazen nudity of the figure, the Queen had it briskly shipped off to what is now the "V&A" (Victoria and Albert) Museum in London. Once there, the museum paid to have a proportionately accurate fig leaf (above) designed to cover David's privates. The Fig Leaf was used only for Queenly visits so as not to further embarrass her Majesty. For those occasions, the leaf was hung on David using two strategically placed hooks. It was then removed upon the departure of Her Royal Highness. Today that same Fig Leaf is kept in a display of its own in the V&A, far and away from David.

Behind the Fig Leaf

This image depicts a before-and-after of the cleaning of this Masaccio fresco entitled "The Expulsion of Adam and Eve." Fig leaves were added three centuries after the original fresco was painted, probably at the request of Cosimo III de' Medici in the late 17th century, who saw nudity as disgusting. During restoration in the 1980's the fig leaves were removed to restore the fresco to its original condition.

217

SANTA MARIA NOVELLA
ART, RELIGION, SCIENCE & CHARIOT RACES
Piazza di Santa Maria Novella, 18, 50123 Firenze

The Dominican Basilica of Santa Maria Novella was first designed in the 1200's by Fra Sisto Fiorentino and Fra Ristoro da Campi. The piazza in front features a rare sight in Florence: a grassy area that fills the center of the piazza in front of the Church. Cosimo I de Medici used this Piazza for Chariot Races in the mid-1500's. He had it set up to imitate an antique Roman circus. The two obelisks rest on bronze tortoises, made in 1608 by the sculptor Giambologna. These obelisks were used by the ancient Romans as timing posts to go around.

Located across the street from the Stazione Santa Maria Novella (train station), it is easy to find and it is not uncommon to see large crowds as people gather for a myriad of festivals, events or simply for an afternoon of shopping from tables of local food and wares.

Look for Important artwork inside:

- Crucifix by Brunelleschi
- Nativity by Botticelli
- Stained Glass Window by Ghirlandaio & Lippi
- Frescoes by Lippi & Uccello
- Trinity by Masaccio
- Painting by Giorgio Vasari

Great website:
www.ChiesaSantaMarianNovella.it

The Easter Eclipse

During the 1570s a local scientist, Ignazio Danti, pierced a hole through the stained glass Rose window. Once every 20 years (or so) a partial eclipse of the moon would coincide with the Vernal Equinox in March, the first day of Spring. At this time, the eclipse would shine through the hole in the window and travel a pre-determined path along the Church floor to let him know the exact date that Easter would occur.

The magnificent interior of the Basilica of Santa Maria Novella is breath-taking with its high vaulted ceilings with heaven-directed pointed buttresses. The decorous pulpit and the crucifix were created by Filippo Brunelleschi (the same man who designed the huge dome on the Duomo), while Sandro Botticelli created the early nativity scene above the door. The frescoes were created by Filippino Lippi, Nardo di Cione and Domenico Ghirlandaio among others. A long list of esteemed artists contributed to different areas, including wood carvings by Baccio D'Agnono and the tombstone of Leonardo Dati was created by Lorenzo Ghiberti and the Madonna of the Rosary is credited to Giorgio Vasari (the Vasari Corridor).

The Quadrant

is used for finding the time by utilizing the sun: The 'horary' quadrant could be used to find the time either in equal or unequal (length of the day divided by twelve) hours. Different sets of markings were created for either equal or unequal hours. For measuring the time in equal hours, the horary quadrant could only be used for one specific latitude while a quadrant for unequal hours could be used anywhere based on an approximate formula. One edge of the quadrant had to be aligned with the sun, and once aligned, a bead on the end of a plumb line attached to the center of the quadrant showed the time of the day. In the late 1500's, the astronomer, mathematician and geographer Egnazio Danti placed two astronomical instruments on the facade of Santa Maria Novella that he used to study the apparent motion of the Sun.

GEMS ~ PLACES

THE ANCIENT PHARMACY
OF SANTA MARIA NOVELLA
Via della Scala 16, 50123 Florence, Italy

Built in 1221 *[nearly 800 years ago!]* by Dominican friars, the pharmacy is an adjunct to the Cathedral of Santa Maria Novella, and over the centries it it spilled out to a shared common area that is surrounded by the living quarters of various friars and monks. In 1661, the Grand Duke of Tuscany, Ferdinando II de' Medici, sponsored the remodelling of the facility and its opening to the general public.

Many of the natural potions and remedies that were concocted here were not only for the use of the Monastery, but many of them eventually came to be the favorites of royals all over Europe.

The "Orange Blossom Water" was the favorite of Catherine de' Medici who often gifted it to her friends on special occasions.

The full range of scents and remedies are known for the quality of creation and the exacting usage of the age-old recipes.

Today, the wide range of products maintains a global following while still using locally-grown ingredients (when they can be found), and they attribute their sterling reputation for their strict standards of exactitude and adherence to traditional methods of manufacturing.

The Pharmacy is a little difficult to find because it has a small sign that lies flat against a nondescript building on a non-touristic street in a regular local neighborhood. But when you find the sign that reads "Officina Profumo," you will open an outer door that takes you

1.

2.

Some of the old tools of the pharmaceutical trade, such as these mortars & pestles, are on display in the Remedy room.

into an entry hall (1). *Fantastico!* A study in Renaissance-style architecture, this entrance will catch you by surprise. Without having yet entered the pharmacy, you will already be pleasantly surprised at the mixture of fragrances that is by now a part of the overall architecture, having been present for centuries. Once inside the main room, you will feel tiny as you gaze up to the gabled ceilings (2) whose space is artistically finished with visual stories of history and lit with regal chandeliers.

Each room offers a visual surprise for you to enjoy. They include a large Fragrance Room (2), an enticing Herbal room (3), and the Herbal Remedy room (or pharmacy) (4). To make a purchase, simply point to the item that you would like, and the proud and friendly clerks will give you a 'voucher' for you to take to the Payment room. Once payment has been made, you will return to this room and the same clerk will give you a nicely packaged version of the item in which you have purchased.

3.

Some of the remedies are still made today. For example, their "Pot Pourri" is still made using locally-grown flowers and essences, and it is fermented in large terra terracotta vats to ferment the same way since the 1200's.

3.

4.

BASILICA DI SANTO SPIRITO

OLTRARNO NEIGHBORHOOD

Piazza Santo Spirito, 30, 50125 Florence

GEMS ~ PLACES

Compared to the other ornately designed churches in Florence, the Basilica di Santo Spirito seems mundane and unobtrusive. But do not let the unadorned façade fool you, for on the inside of this lackluster church, exists one of the most divine spiritual interiors in Florence.

Designed in 1434 by Filippo Brunelleschi (the genius that created the Duomo), it was commissioned to replace the 13th century convent that had previously burned down. Brunelleschi's plans were not followed entirely by the barrage of architects and builders because, alas, Brunelleschi died before proceeding further than the design phase of this Church. For example, Brunelleschi had originally envisioned a barrel-vaulted nave and a façade with four doors. But by the time the structure was consecrated in 1481, it was clear that his wishes were ignored. The nave was built with a flat ceiling and the façade consisted of the more traditional three-door approach. Filippo felt that the entire structure and piazza should be reversed so that the piazza would open out to the Arno River. In his mind, the beauty of the Basilica would attract

> Soon after the consecration of the church, the Prior asked the young Michelangelo to carve a crucifix from wood. In order to get this accomplished, he had to provide a room for Michelangelo to live in while working at the Basilica. It was in this room that Michelangelo was known to have brought cadavers, so that he could study the goings-on beneath the skin. He was determined to understand why people look the way they look, and he felt he could glean this understanding no other way.

everyone who walked along the river. But several local residents refused to move their homes, so this too was ignored.

Over the centuries, the building was subjected to a multitude of changes, but it still retains the underpinnings of Brunelleschi's genius. This includes the majestic colonnade of Corinthian influence, and the thirty-eight niches that contain a variety of private and family chapels. Giorgio Vasari: "if all of those people would have left Brunelleschi's original design alone, this Basilica would have been the most perfect church in all of Christendom. As it stands it is at least more charming and better proportioned than any other."

The decorous interior of
the Basilica di Santo Spiri-
to is a surprise after seeing the
rather plain exterior. A wonderful
thing to see is Michelangelo's
wooden Crucifix. Walk around it
to give yourself the full impact of
this impeccable work accom-
plished by Florence's favorite
young genius.

PLACES ~ GEMS

Fun to Do While Enjoying a Gelato

After your visit to the Basilica di Santo Spirito, exit to the piazza outside. On the left you'll notice a line-up of eateries. Just past them on the left ~ providing you find yourself able to ignore the enticing aromas emanating from those stylish restaurants ~ you'll see a small gelato store. Go inside (there are two rooms to enjoy) and look at the walls: covering the walls you will find hundreds of artistic versions of the face of the Basilica. Artists, children, friends and neighbors created their own vision of a decorated facade for Santo Spirito, and the proprietors covered the walls of their gelato store with these visions. It is fun to see each person's individual vision of the face of the Church. While you are there, enjoy your favorite gelato flavor while perusing each of these fun and highly creative little gems of local art.

The Piazza

The Basilica di Santo Spirito is in the Oltrarno neighborhood. This vicinity is outside of the main historic district of Florence and therefore it is a local and authentically Florentine neighborhood. You many not find many folks that speak your own language, but you will find that this piazza is a popular hang-out for young college-aged singles who enjoy a vibrant night life. And of course, the food is fantastico!

Things to See in Santo Spirito

- Wooden Crucifix *by Michelangelo*
- "Madonna and Child" *by Filippo Lippi*
- The Colonnade of tall pillars that shoot your eyes toward the heavens
- A variety of works *by Cosimo Rosselli, Francesco Botticini, Francesco Granacci, Michele Ridolfi,* **Domenico Ghirlandaio,** *Alessandro Allori, and Maso di Banco*

WANDERING AROUND
TODAY'S FLORENCE

WALLS and DOORS

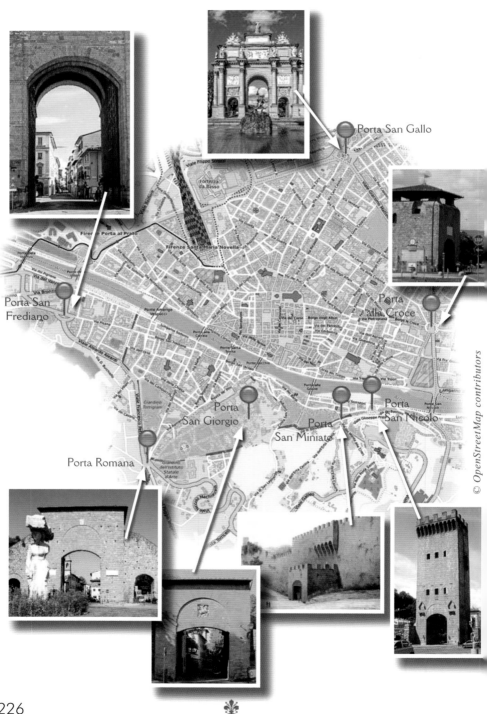

Porta San Gallo

Porta San Frediano

Porta alla Croce

Porta San Giorgio

Porta San Miniato

Porta San Nicolo

Porta Romana

© OpenStreetMap contributors

WANDERING AROUND TODAY

The Walls & Doors ('Portas') of medieval Florence are often overlooked in many of the books that talk about the city. The walls (the pale orange line around the historical district) will give you an idea of the diminutive size of the old city. The battles, the stories, the loves and the losses that have occurred inside - or because of - these walls are forever engraved in the Florentine historic backdrop. When walking the ancient walls, the antiquity is readily felt. And, if you are a runner, the walls are a fantastic 7.7-mile (12.5km) route. The doors may seem oddly placed and spaced, but it is important to remember that they were built during different times for different regimes. Many of the original doors are long gone, and some newer doors seem to be too close to others.

Porta San Gallo is located in the Piazza della Libertà, directly adjacent the picturesque Arch of Triumph (pictured left). The keys to this giant door, built in 1285, are today kept in the Florence Historical & Topographical museum.

Porta alla Croce is located in Piazza Beccaria. Its design is attributed to Arnolfo di Cambi in 1284, and it marks the spot where the first Florentine martyr, San Miniato, was beheaded.

Porta San Niccolo, a fourteenth century gate, is the only remaining tower that was not shortened. This was because the hill of San Miniato provided natural protection from enemy artillery. It is considered to be the most beautiful of the doors today, recently restored.

Porta San Miniato is the only door that has no watch tower. Built in 1320, its independent charm is derived largely from the fact that it was created as simply a hole in the wall that provided less-used access to and from the city.

Porta San Giorgio was built in the fourteenth century with a much taller tower than the one you will see today. In the early sixteenth century, nearly 200 years after its construction, Michelangelo was put in charge of the city's fortifications, and chose to have the tower shortened to make it less vulnerable under fire.

Porta Romana, a massive statement of the troubled fourteenth century, is beautifully restored and preserved. The most direct portal when traveling between Rome and Florence, this gate faces southward toward Rome, hence its name. A modern statue of two women has created local controversy as they stand watch in the round-about just outside the door. In 1515, a Medici crest was placed over the door to commemorate the arrival of Pope Leo X (one of the Medici Popes) from Rome.

Porta San Frediano, designed in the 1330's by Andrea Pisano, is the Western-most door to the city of Florence. Like the other city doors (with the exception of Porta San Niccolo), Porta San Frediano was shortened in the sixteenth century during Michelangelo's management of city fortifications. This robust structure still has its original massive wooden doors, complete with its ancient bolts. On the outside of the wall, you will find iron rings embedded in the wall. Visitors to the city would tie their horses to these rings, entering the city on foot.

Many parts of the original wall around the city are no longer in existence; as they eroded over time, they were replaced with more modern features of the city.

Today's Florence is substantially larger than the Old City. Outside of the old wall dwells a very modern business district (north), the Florence Airport, the University of Florence, the Stadium and many more modern amenities and neighborhoods inhabited by today's happy Florentines.

What's a Piazza?

A "Piazza" quite simply is a town square. There are over 60 piazzas in Florence, and they serve as post-Mass gathering places, social events, business functions, performances, political protests, parties, and simply as hang-outs.

Often a piazza will feature canopy-covered tables & restaurants so diners can enjoy their meal 'al fresco' (in the fresh air), see their neighbors passing by, or to be seen by all the right people. And sometimes a piazza may simply function as an open parking lot.

Before or after church, masses of people can be seen socializing in a piazza. In the afternoon, it is not unusual to see many students hanging out enjoying the incredibly colorful and wide selections of gelato found in many piazzas. In the evening, the whole feeling of the piazza may change as folks come out for dinner, and entertainers come out to perform for the locals and the tourists alike.

piazzas are a wonderful place for art, as you will often see beautiful sculptures and fountains dominating a piazza. Artists love the piazzas to exhibit their paintings, drawings, sculptures and crafts.

When visiting Italy, Americans commonly gravitate to a nearby piazza because these spaces feel wide open and alive with fun sights for the eyes, sounds for the ears, and a mass of beautiful people ready to start a conversation with a friendly "Ciao!"

List of Piazzas in Florence

Piazza del Duomo <
Piazza della Repubblica <
Piazza Santa Croce <
Piazza della Signoria <
Piazza San Lorenzo <
Piazza Santa Maria Novella <
Piazza della Santissima Annunziata
Piazza della Stazione <
Piazza dell'Indipendenza <
Piazza San Marco <
Piazza Santa Trinita <
Piazza dei Ciompi
Piazza d'Azeglio
Piazza Goldoni
Piazza del Limbo <
Piazza dei Giudici
Piazza Mentana
Piazza del Mercato Centrale <
Piazza Ognissanti <
Piazza delle Pallottole Il Prato
Piazza San Benedetto
Piazza San Firenze <
Piazza San Pier Maggiore
Piazza Strozzi <
Piazza dell'Unità Italiana
Piazza del Capitolo
Piazza Adua
Piazza Beccaria
Piazza di Giovanni <
Piazza de la Lanzi <
Piazza della Libertà <
Piazzale Donatello <

Pictured here is "Piazza Santa Trinita."

Piazza Bambine e Bambini di Beslan
Piazza Oberdan
Piazza Puccini
Piazza San Jacopino <
Piazza Savonarola <
Piazza della Vittoria
Piazza Vittorio Veneto
Piazza Piave
Piazza Dalmazia
Piazza Leopoldo Pietro
Piazza del Carmine <
Piazza di Cestello
Piazza Demidoff
Piazzale Michelangelo <
Piazza de' Mozzi
Piazza Piattellina <
Piazza de' Pitti <
Piazza Giuseppe Poggi
Piazza Santo Spirito <
Piazza Tasso <
Piazza del Tiratoio
Piazza della Passera
Piazza Santa Maria Soprarno <
Piazza de' Nerli <
Piazzale di Porta Romana<
Piazza San Felice <
iazza della Calza <
Piazza del Pesce <
Piazza Torquato Tasso <
Piazza degli Alberghi <
Piazza de Cimatori <

POPULAR PIAZZAS
Piazza della Signoria...

enjoys the prestige of being the historical and political heart of Florence. Lined with a yummy selection of cafes and restaurants, visitors enjoy sitting at the outdoor tables enjoying the gelato-bearing convoy as much as the famously nectarous Tuscan wines.

Within its bounds is the Loggia dei Lanzi *(right)*, as well as the entrance to the crenellated and foreboding Palazzo Vecchio. Outside of the Palazzo's front door is an array of statuary that is clearly second to none. First and foremost is the enigmatic Michelangelo's elegant and perfect statue of "David." The most famous statue in the World. *(This is a copy - the original "David" is in Florence's Galleria dell'Accademia.)* Next to David stands "Hercules and Cacus" by Baccio Bandinelli, with its strong image of the tiumphant over the defeated.

Along the face of the building is Donatello's ultra-emotional "Judith and Holofernes." *(This too is a copy, as the original can be found inside the Palazzo Vecchio.)* In the "Fountain of Neptune" by Bartolomeo Ammannati, Neptune possesses the face of Cosimo I de' Medici. And speaking of Cosimo I, Giambologna's "Equestrian Statue of Cosimo I" rides tall near the fountain as it represents the pride of military victory. In the ground in front of the "Fountain of Neptune" is the memorial plaque in the spot where Fra Girolamo Savonarola was tortured, hanged then burned.

Ceremonies, festivals, live performers and speech-givers can all be found the Piazza della Signoria for your enjoyment. One of life's rare treats: this piazza is free to admire 24/7. Just for kicks, pay it a visit at night when the lights give the statuary - and the whole piazza - an entirely different 'personality.'

Loggia dei Lanzi

Savonarola's Plaque

Palazzo Vecchio

"David"

"Fountain of Neptune"

Loggia dei Lanzi

Along the west side of the Piazza della Signoria is the splendid Loggia dei Lanzi (or the Loggia della Signoria, or the Loggia dell'Orcagna, all depending on the ruler of the day), a vast and permanent outdoor sculpture gallery. This entire piazza has seen a multitude of civic leaders and functions. Completed in 1382 by Benci di Cione and Simone di Francesco Talenti, it was originally created to stage an extensive palette of colorful civic events intended for public consumption.

The Loggia includes four broad arches, three of which open to the Piazza della Signoria, and the fourth faces toward the Piazza degli Uffizi. Between the tops of the arches are allegorical symbols of the four cardinal virtues of Fortitude, Temperance, Justice and Prudence created by Agnolo Gaddi in 1380.

During the 1500's, the Loggia became a symbol of Medici power and was changed into the largest outdoor gallery in the world. The statues were not placed according to popularity, but like everything else in those days, they were strategically placed to send specific messages of power and victory. On the roof, a decorative terrace garden was dreamed up by Buontalenti to become the place where the Medici could enjoy the many public functions from a position of safety.

Along the rear wall are six female statues that were brought to Florence from Rome in 1789, while the two Lions on the steps are indisputable representatives of the city of Florence herself.

Perseus
Cellini

The
Rape of
Polyxena
Pio Fedi

Menelaus
supporting
the body of
Patroclus
Ancient Roman

Hercules
beating the
Centaur
Nessus
Giambologna

Rape of
the Sabine
Women
Giambologna

WANDERING AROUND TODAY

GETTING HIGH in FLORENCE
THE BEST PLACES FOR THE BEST PHOTOS

WANDERING AROUND TODAY

Camera buffs, THIS is for YOU!

If photography is of interest to you, then you know how important it is to find good angles from which to shoot. Most guidebooks have terrific photos, but they don't often let you know from where they were shot. These are a few of the places where you can climb up to take many of the photos in this book. Notice how from above, this city appears to be surprisingly ancient. As you can see, a picturesque palette awaits your climb. Some may require you to purchase a ticket, some are free, and some may require you to purchase a glass of local vino!   ;-)

But no matter which you choose, you will enjoy this rare perspective into the ancient past from above.

Climb to the top of Giotto's Bell Tower next door to see an up-close view of Brunelleschi's great master creation, il Duomo.

If you decide to scale the 414  *steps to the top of the Campanile (Giotto's Bell Tower) you can see all of Florence. Across the Piazza is the majestic Duomo, complete with it's own viewing cupola that is the crown of the city. Looking down, it is easy to imagine that you are looking back through time to the ancient past.*

From atop the north side of the Campanile, you can look down on the eight-sided Baptistery in the foreground, and further away you can see another dome: the Cappella de' Medici (the Medici Chapel) resting quietly in the near distance.

WANDERING AROUND TODAY

WANDERING AROUND TODAY

Looking southwest from the top of the crenellated tower of the Palazzo Vecchio, you will acquire a terrific view of the Bargello. Initially built as a seat for law enforcement, it later became an infamous prison where from its crenellations, you might have seen a few bodies dangling upside down as a direct message to those that might wish to break the law.

Looking down from the Palazzo Vecchio tower, a spectacular view of the Piazza de la Signoria and the Loggia dei Lanzi await you. Many days, this is one of the more peopled piazzas in the city.

◀ *After climbing a mere 223 steps to the top of the Palazzo Vecchio tower, a feast for your eyes awaits you at every single rest level where tiny windows give you a break and a glimpse of what lies below you.*

Looking southward, the main scenic feature is the Church of Santa Croce. With a large piazza out front (as with many churches), you will find musicians and street performers of every kind. But inside is where all the bodies are buried - literally. From a Dante cenotaph to Donatello, and from Florence Nightingale to Michelangelo, this church has become the final resting place for many famous folks. And to top it off, it is adorned with a smattering of della Robbia's shiny and unique terracotta sculptures. ▼

WANDERING AROUND TODAY

PIAZZALE MICHELANGELO
The Post Card View

Piazzale Michelangelo *is a medium-effort walk from the Ponte Vecchio Bridge. But whether you hike it or you take the #12 Bus up the hill, be sure to bring a picnic basket. This is one of the more popular places to end your day and to watch the sun set over the city.*

This view, taken from atop the Westin Excelsior Hotel on the Arno River (Piazza Ognissanti, 3, Firenze) is clearly fantastico! Day or night, rain or shine, this panorama is quite a sight to behold. Take the elevator to the top (8th) floor, go through the bar and out the glass doors to get this sumptuous feast for your eyes. The 8th floor doesn't seem very high, but when you are in an ancient city where most structures are a mere 2-3 stories, 8 floors is plenty high!

Capella Medici
(Medici Chapel)

il Duomo & il Campanile di Giotto
(the Dome & Giotto's Bell Tower)

WANDERING AROUND TODAY

▲ **Hotel La Scaletta** *is a gem in a hidden treasure chest! A bit tough to find: Once you have located the correct building (near the Pitti Palace) you will climb a few steps, take a rickety little 2-person eleva-tor to the top, walk through a small lobby into a restaurant, go out the back door, up some steps to a roof-top bar, then up one more precarious narrow flight to the rooftop. There you will find a couple of small cafe tables waiting for you to savor the wine & cheese along with these fantastic views of the historical center of the city, and the Observatory over Boboli Gardens behind you (inset). A VERY romantic way to enjoy the sunset. (Hotel La Scaletta: Via Guicciardini, 13 - 50125 FLORENCE)*

Getting High in Firenze: **More Places to Climb Up to Look Down**

The Bargello Museum

Palazzo Vecchio (Old Palace)

Piazzale Michelangelo

Hotel La Scaletta

239

WANDERING AROUND TODAY

ARNO RIVER

7 bridges span the Arno River in Florence (west to east): Ponte delle Cascine, Ponte Amerigo Vespucci, Ponte Alle Carraia, Ponte Santa Trinità, **Ponte Vecchio** Ponte Alle Grazie, and Ponte de San Niccolò.

In 1966, the Arno experienced its worst flood since the 1500's. Over 4 million books and 14,000 masterpieces were damaged or lost completely.

After the flood of 1966, volunteers from around the globe came to dig Florence out of the mud. These wonderful volunteers became affectionately known by the locals as the "Angeli del Fango" or "Mud Angels."

> The Santa Trinità Bridge was built by Bartolomeo Ammannati, who was inspired by Michelangelo.
>
> Scavenger boats were known to scrape the river bottom in search of ancient pillars, bricks and metals that, for various reasons, were lost in the river. They were collected in order to restore some of the buildings along the river to an older, or more original state.

Halfway across The Ponte alle Grazie Bridge, you will find this contemporary amusing statue of a man walking off of the bridge. Fun photo opp!

The picturesque Arno River, with its tumultuous and emotional history, is considered to be one of the more treasured scenes in Europe. With a varied history of war-torn decimation of her bridges and destruction-causing floods, the Arno continues to bounce back to the widely-loved river of romance that continues to be enjoyed - and cherished - today.

WANDERING AROUND TODAY

FINDING ART TODAY

Art, art, everywhere art. Florence boasts the existence of more art schools than any other city in the world. Because of the huge population of great artists that have lived throughout her history, art seeps from every crevice, everywhere you look in Florence. There is no such thing as a boring gelato display, or a plain old shoe store with shoes all lined in nice rows. Everything has been designed or put together with a discerning artistic eye. When wandering around Florence, peer into windows and peek into doorways. You will be rewarded with a magnificent array of creative displays of just about everything in the city. You'll see cobblers happily hand-making those beautiful Italian leather shoes and handbags, clock makers creating clocks of every type and style, sculpture schools where the students' products are available for purchase, and mono-lens-wearing jewelers who pride themselves in their discovery of new ways to use gold and stones. There is a volume of sculptures and carvings that you'll be hard-pressed to match anywhere. And you will find paintings and frescoes around every single turn. In no other city in the world will you find such a proliferation of art than in talent-rich global center of art, Florence.

Who was the Mysterious Berta?

It is said that a witch cast a spell that turned this woman to stone. On the other hand, it is also said that Berta was a lonely woman that asked the church of Santa Maria Maggiore to ring a bell at the end of the day to tell the homeless outside to come inside the walls before the gates close for the night. Either way, you will find Berta on the outer wall of the Church of Santa Maria Maggiore.

Art is EVERYWHERE and in every form. A 'Duomo' umbrella is not difficult to find; this lady holding her nose is in a local neighborhood above where they used to keep the trash piles (in the old days). She is someone's statement of the stinkiness! You'll find her up on a wall at the NW corner of Borgo San Jacobo and Via Tuscanella.

(vertical text, left margin) WANDERING AROUND TODAY

STREET ART

Florence is the most artistically inspirational city in the world. It has more art schools and artists per square inch than any other city in the world. Here, artists are raised among the masters and are taught by emulating these masters. Then in turn, they are constantly challenged to surpass them altogether.

There are areas in the main streets of the historical district of Florence where the city has reserved areas in which the local artists can create something amazing on a large scale and under the critical eyes of the masses. To stand in the street with a gelato in your hand while you watch their pieces come alive is truly a unique and magical Florentine experience. Sadly, when you walk past these places the next day, they will all be gone, replaced by new public art-for-a-day street art projects. Again, this is a truly unique Florentine experience that will surely amaze, impress and delight your visual senses. Do not leave this city without enjoying this little gift from Florence!

A local artist, left, begins his day with chalk in hand. Below, a sizeable group of artists recreate Leonardo da Vinci's globally famous "Last Supper."

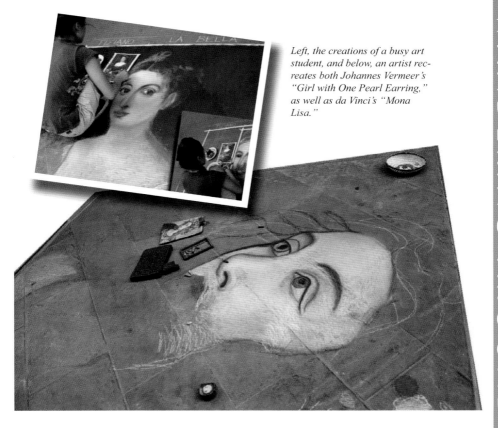

Left, the creations of a busy art student, and below, an artist recreates both Johannes Vermeer's "Girl with One Pearl Earring," as well as da Vinci's "Mona Lisa."

WANDERING AROUND TODAY

SIGNS OF THE TIMES

It seems that after enjoying the wold's best art for centuries, today's artists may find it difficult to acquire a unique style, to be heard - or seen. French-born street Artist Clet Abraham has wandered through Florence, Rome and Paris re-making city street signs. As you meander your way around Florence, each sign will bring a smile your face every time you round a corner to see where you are. They are prevalent and creative. Enjoy spreading the word about Clet and his marvelous senses of irony and humor at:

https://www.facebook.com/clet.abraham and
https://instagram.com/cletabraham

Easy Opera

If you consider yourself to be an Opera 'lightweight,' this is a great way to see an Italian Opera. It's fast, it's small, and it is within walking distance from most hotels in Florence. On the Oltrarno side of the River is the Anglican Church of St. Mark's. It is a local Church with a real 'neighborhood' feeling. They provide live operatic and concert entertainment for anyone that is interested in walking through their door. It is an intimate little venue with the cavernous acoustics that only a church can provide. There are few easier ways in the world to savor a dramatic Italian opera. Tickets can be purchased in advance, in person or **online**. The experience will be truly local, authentic and memorable.

St Mark's • Via Maggio 16, 50125 Firenze, Italy
http://stmarksitaly.com • (Int + 39) 055 294 764

WANDERING AROUND TODAY

Fun Activity

How many can you find? Kids love to run around the city (escorted, of course) to see how many of these signs they can find, and take a selfie in front of them. It is a fun and creative activity to teach them about contemporary art, how to read signs, or simply to explore the wonderful city of Firenze!

Fun Activity

The Central Mercato will delight all of your senses. This is the place where the local markets and restaurants go to purchase all of their fresh foods each day. It opens around 4am and may be closed early in the afternoon. Zillions of stalls that offer sweets, meats and treats. Some will serve you, and some will pack a sack for you. In any case, be prepared to be embraced by a symphony of aromas, and an orchestra of superb sights and flavors. Yummm!

Mercato Centrale 50123 Florence
http://www.mercatocentrale.it/mercato-centrale-firenze

WANDERING AROUND TODAY

FIESOLE
ETRUSCAN & ROMAN RUINS

ARCHAEOLOGY in FIESOLE
A DAY TRIP

The Etruscans occupied this area as far back as 800 bce. By the early 100's ce, the Romans had not only taken over, but they had begun to build structures - sometimes over the top of the original Etruscan ruins. Fiesole was likely desired by the Romans because of its strategic hilltop location with excellent views of possible incoming enemies. Oftentimes it served as a weekend get-away for wealthy Florentines like the Medici.

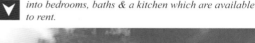

The town of Fiesole main-tains its charming Tuscan style. A stroll through the town will yield a nice selection of restaurants with a view of Florence and a delightful array of shops.

A 3,000-seat Roman Theatre nestles comfortably, and to this day performances are still enjoyed here. The medieval bell tower in the background (the campanile) is called "Casalta." Once an ovile (sheep pen) and a barn, it has been converted into bedrooms, baths & a kitchen which are available to rent.

WANDERING AROUND TODAY

When they needed a break  *from the day-to-day issues of the city, the Medici family would escape to their hilltop villa in nearby Fiesole.*

The town of Fiesole is the perfect 'day trip' from Florence. Simply hop on Bus#7 and ride it to its end (approx 9 miles). Welcome to Fiesole! While there, take time to visit the staggering ancient ruins (courtesy of the Etruscans, and later the Romans), and the vista over the entire city of Florence. Bus#7 will get you back to Florence in time for dinner.

Near the main bus stop you will find a very long ramp that leads up to the hilltop. After the climb, your efforts will be rewarded with this phenomenal panoramic overview of Florence.

251

ETRUSCAN & ROMAN RUINS
and Museum

The wonderful site museum exhibits works of ancient art as well as the bodies of a few of her ancient people, some of which have been examined using today's advanced equipment and medical experts. Did they suffer from the same ailments a couple of thousand years ago as we do today? ▼

The Romans called the area "Etrurea," and the locals they called the "Etruscans." This is where the words "Tuscany" and "Tuscans" originated from.

The arches of the Roman baths frame the modern bell tower (campanile) in the distance. ▷

After a walk through the ruins, you can grab a bite in the cafe on the grounds that overlooks these beautiful ruins. Do not miss the museum: a beautiful job was done in the telling of the stories of the ancients who once roamed this scenic spot.

WANDERING AROUND TODAY

Who were the Etruscans?

The Etruscans were an ancient population that existed from 700BCE to 300BCE, when they were conquered by the Romans. They had a language and a culture all their own, with a complex social structure that included the arts as well as a monetary system.

Because actual original texts of philosophy or religion ~ or of everyday life, for that matter ~ do no exist, we have only the anecdotal writings of ancient Roman folks like Pliny the Elder and Herodotus to tell us the stories of the Etruscans.

This, in actual fact, is where it all began.

The end. REALLY.

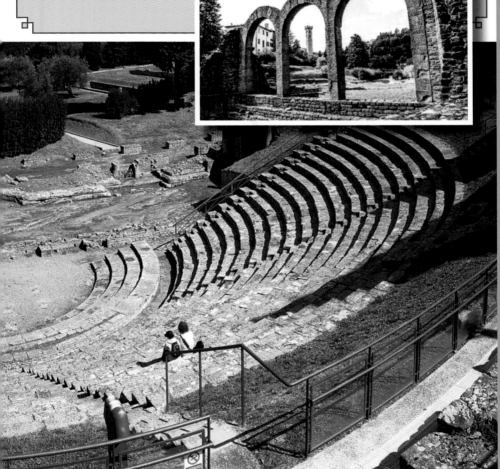

BACKGROUND

SUMMARY

Now that you have met some of the most accomplished and curious minds in human history, and you have visited the museums of the city that illustrate their stories, it might be a good time to attempt an explanation of how the Renaissance could possibly have occurred in Florence. It seems there were a number of simultaneous events in play, each adding its own timber to a growing flame:

- The lack of a strong well-established governmental system

- The previously strong and controlling religion was at a faltering point

- The Black Death plague caused people to flee the walls, where they met new people from the 'outside' who told their stories of a completely different kind of life

- The discovery then diligent pursuit of ancient writings that described an altogether different way of life began to permeate the consciousness

- The literary promotion of 'free thinking' stemmed from the discovery of the ancient writings of Lucretius, Cicero and other Roman and Greek philosophers, creating a new attitude of human value

- The adoption of the belief that every person is important: *Humanism*

- The creation of the printing press quickly spread new ideas, and boosted the demand for educated readers and writers

- A curiosity whose power would reshape social and religious limitations found a financial buttress

- An educated appreciation of the arts; an unusually strong sense of competition among the creative population - the hard-core competition to out-do not only their peers but their masters as well

- The unexpected means of expression that became the 'voice' of change: *Art*

- Funds had to be readily available in vast portions to promote the education and the creation of new kinds of art; money had to be poured into hundreds, nay thousands of artists like never before - or since - in order to produce this handful of Giants

All of these elements collided spontaneously to create an exploding social support that encouraged - rather than squelched - the citizens to break free of the mind-numbing control of the Middle Ages.

The result was one of the most compelling, provocative and expressive eras of the expansion of the human spirit in all of history, the one we now call the Renaissance.

Recommended Reading

"The Swerve"
~Stephen Greenblatt

"Lives of the Artists"
~Giorgio Vasari

"The Prince"
~ Niccolo Machiavelli

"Divine Comedy"
~ Dante Alighieri

"Life of Michelangelo Buonarotti"
~ Charles Holroyd

"Autobiography"
~ Benvenito Cellini"

"Life of Brunelleschi"
~ Antonio Manetti

"The House of Medici - Its Rise and Fall"
~ Christopher Hibbert

"Tuscan Sculptors: Their Lives and Works"
~ Charles Callahan Perkins

"Inferno"
~ Dan Brown

Websites

www.DavinciMuseum.it

KhanAcademy.com

NationalGeographic.com

www.MuseoGalileo.it

www.Piazza-Signoria.com

NGA.gov
National Gallery of Art

Videos

"The Medici - Godfathers of the Renaissance"
~ Tsenka Stoycheva

"The Great Cathedral Mystery"
~ National Geographic

"How an Amateur Built the World's Biggest Dome"
~ National Geographc

"Florence Artisans"
~ National Geographic

INDEX

BACKGROUND

BACKGROUND

ABOUT THE AUTHOR

Patty Civalleri is a lifelong historian and an acknowledged armchair archaeologist. As a founding member of the Director's Council of the prestigious Cotsen Institute of Archaeology at UCLA, a professional photographer, and a writer, she has traveled the globe for 15 years with world-renowned archaeologists to document ancient cultures from some of the deepest corners of our historical past. Throughout those years she has written articles and photographed for the Institute's respected and award-winning annual archaeological journal, for travel guides and a wide variety of business publications.

Civalleri resides in Southern California where she, her husband Roger and their son Jason enjoy sailing to Catalina Island aboard their family's sailboat. She loves cooking, archaeology, working in clay, singing, playing classical piano, the symphony, and a hyperactive social life.

Visit FlorenceTravelBook.com *to be informed as new books are released!*